THE ULTIMATE EXPERIENCE

THE MANY PATHS TO GOD

THE TEACHINGS of the

MASTERS of LIGHT

Presenters: Our Father-Christ Michael, Lord Yeshua, Lady Nada, Divine Mother, Lord Kuthumi, AA Michael, Blue Star the Pleiadian, Mary Magdalene, Earth Mother Gaia, Mahatma Buddha, Lady Guinevere, Archangel Metatron, Lord Ashtar, Lord Enoch, Lord Sananda, Goddess Quan Yin, Sanat Kumara, and Andromeda Rex.

BOOK SEVEN

Verling CHAKO Priest, Ph.D.

*To Barbara —
Enjoy the fruits of
my labor !
Love,
Chako
11-10-09*

Trafford PUBLISHING® www.trafford.com

North America & international
toll-free: 1 888 232 4444 (USA & Canada)
phone: 250 383 6864 ♦ fax: 250 383 6804 ♦ email: info@trafford.com

The United Kingdom & Europe
phone: +44 (0)1865 487 395 ♦ local rate: 0845 230 9601
facsimile: +44 (0)1865 481 507 ♦ email: info.uk@trafford.com

10 9 8 7 6 5 4 3 2 1

DEDICATION

I dedicate this Book SEVEN to God and

The many Masters who teach us:

God hath not given us the spirit of fear,

But of power, and of love,

And of a sound mind (2 Timothy 1:7)

ACKNOWLEDGMENTS

Dear Readers, once again it is time for me to express my deepest appreciation to those who have helped me in creating this Book SEVEN. Foremost, my heartfelt thanks need to be given to God and all of His Helpers—the many Ascended Masters, Goddesses, and Archangels. Their loving Teachings and Remarks set the tone of this book.

Heather Clarke, who is not only the founder of the Arizona Enlightenment Center in Goodyear, is my friend as well as my Editor. When I first started writing my books, I knew I would need an editor. *Ask and yea shall receive!* Heather walked into my life and has been a most valuable component of these books. In other words, I could not have done it without you, dear soul. Thank you.

My oldest daughter, Susan Verling Miller O'Brien, is also an invaluable member of my team. Once I have completed all of the channeling and I have transcribed the 13 tapes (ninety minutes each), I email all of the files to her and she frames the book, cover to cover, creates the Table of Contents, and so forth. This is "grunt work" she never complains about and strives to complete the tasks in a timely fashion. It pays to have a Virgo on your team! Susan is detail-oriented and does a superb job. Thank you, heart of my heart.

Readers, a book is not successful if no one will read it. Therefore, I give my heartfelt appreciation to all of you who love the books and keep coming back for the next one and the next one... Blessings.

PREFACE

It all seems so long ago when the Lord Sananda literally came to me and gently stroked my cheek, making that first contact in order to awaken me to my tasks at hand. That was in 2002, and I have barely looked back since.

I believe that when a person repeatedly performs a task, that person is being guided to fulfill a contract for soul— whether it is to transmute energy or it is to carry forth abilities from the past. I have had several past lives where I was a prolific writer—a journalist, a scribe, and author of many letters during Biblical times. Since in this present era it is our soul's endeavor to bring its past lives forward in order to transmute the dark edges and garner the wisdom from the experiences, it is only natural that my past talents have surfaced in this lifetime.

Each time that I experience that familiar emotion that someone has connected to my heart and wishes to communicate, I joyously respond, after checking him out to be sure he is who he says he is. It was in March 2008 that I was asked to start sitting in order to bring in our next book. Therefore, on Friday, the 28th at 10:15 AM, the work actually started.

This book was delivered in a more laid-back fashion in that I only channeled two or three times per week. This gave me more time to transcribe the tapes and to participate in other activities without feeling I ought to be "sitting."

I am never given the secondary title until they have given me several sessions, simply because the title can change. However, after a few transmissions, it became clear to me that the emphasis for this book would be on the Teachings of the various Masters. This is always fun for me as I get to experience all the different Energies from them as well as to receive their Messages. I was continuously surprised at the variety of the 18 Presenters, let alone their interesting topics—from Lord Kuthumi's narrative of homosexual planets to Lady Guinevere's Camelot.

The Masters are still emphasizing the importance of revisiting our belief systems, being flexible, and the willingness to change. Since this year of 2008 is an important election year for America, the Masters often make remarks about the election from their perspective. This book is biased in that their observations seem to favor Senator Obama, as do I. Therefore, keep an opened mind and vote from your heart and your consciousness—with whomever *you* resonate.

My hope for you Readers is that you will first honor these Teachings from the beloved Masters, to acknowledge what a privilege it is for us to receive their wisdom. In the days of Antiquity, this interaction was not possible, except for a small number of magnificent Prophets who had raised their vibratory rate high enough in order to be able to receive the Teachings. Now this contact is available to all of humanity if it would only set the intent.

I urge you not to read this book from cover to cover in one or two sittings. Take the time to reflect on what has been said and see how you can interact from your heart. I hope you enjoy this work as much as I did in receiving it.

FOREWORD

Good morning one and all on this beautiful day in Arizona on Friday, March 28, 2008, at 10:15 AM. I am making contact with this beautiful Conduit, this Channel known to all who read these books as *Chako*. We are a blend. We are a blend of the energies of the Most High.

We are Saint Germain; we are Yeshua; we are Sananda; we are Ashtar and we are God, your Father. We come this day to tell you that we are now ready to proceed with our next task—our next book that so many of you have eagerly been awaiting. It is Book SEVEN and the book list continues to grow.

This is a *Foreword* to the book and not an *Introduction* as yet, for there is much that we wish to say before we start the actual book. As you know, the world is going through a great transformation and as she struggles to maintain balance that humanity has distorted for her, she struggles to reach the fifth dimension but has not made it yet. There must be many changes before that is to happen. When we say *changes,* we mean changes in the topography, changes in humanity's consciousness, changes in the love-hate ratio, and changes in the Light-dark ratio. All of this needs to change.

On the physical note, there must be changes in your government. There must be changes in your banking systems and there must be changes among your diplomats, among your people who decide war—who decide who is going to kill whom. This must cease! This must cease for this Earth, Gaia, is struggling to reach those higher dimensions. Humanity has not learned yet to stay in its heart. Now we know there are millions of people—and yes, we say *millions*—who carry Light in their hearts—good people.

But you see, humanity mixes up the perception of *good* with *religion*. If you are very religious and join the choir and/ or do all the things that are required of church members— church tithing, etcetera—then humanity looks upon you as a *good person*. But dear Readers, nothing could be further from the truth.

For the good people of whom we are speaking—the Lightweavers who do something with their Light—it is not religion that carries them forth. It is spirituality. It is their Christ Consciousness which is, of course, *love*. Many of the religious people, the Fundamentalists and I am speaking of all religions where the people become so zealous in their belief systems and their way of thinking, yet will not change this for they are so righteous in those beliefs.

As we have said in the previous books, so much of what humanity believes is religion is not truth. **True spirituality holds no religion over another.** Do you hear this? Did you read this? In true spirituality no religion is held higher than another. I am speaking of Presbyterians, Catholics, Jews, and Islamic. None of your religions is *the* way! Mormon, Pentecostal, Baptist—none of those religions is *the* way. (*Methodists, Episcopalians can be part of that list also including many not mentioned.*)

The only true way is the love of God, the love of Mother God, the love of self in a selfless way, and the love of your Highest Self. We are not speaking of lower ego but only of the Higher Self, the direct attachment to God. **The way, Readers, is Christ Consciousness, totally non-religious.** Christ was associated with Christianity, but Christ Consciousness is for everyone. A Jew can have Christ Consciousness, although many Jews may slam shut this book and go screaming away from it; but it is truth.

Having Christ Consciousness is walking in God's Light, having a 100% love and Light in your physical body, having 100% spiritual awareness. The Christ that you all associate with that name is the man you call *Christ Jesus.* There was no man of that name. There was Yeshua/Sananda. He was Christ. Buddha was Christ. Moses carried the Christ Energy. Mohammad carried the Christ Energy. Sai Baba, the Avatar of India, is a Christ. We are speaking of a belief system where you associate the title Christ as pertaining only to Christianity and that is erroneous down to the last letter. It is totally erroneous.

We are a blend this morning. We blend with the Higher Energies. We blend with Creation. We blend with Mother Earth. We blend with the Elements. We blend with all of you. You have heard so many times that we are one, but it is true, for we all came forth from Creator God. Some day you will meet that other half of you where we divided ourselves and your true Twin Ray will come back to you.

This book that we will be creating together will again have the theme of waking you up, presenting new ideas. In the previous books, we talked about religion versus spirituality. We talked about dimensional divisions. We talked about your space Brothers and Sisters of the Ashtar Command. There are many other Commands throughout the Universes. All the great planets and star systems, the Pleiades, Arcturus, Sirius, each has its Commands, to name but a few.

Everyone at the moment is focused on Earth, for she is a beautiful planet and is special to many of us. As she rises up and the dark ones fight harder, there will be times, humanity, when you may feel that God has forsaken you. However, remember that God is in each person's heart, including the dark ones. He has never forsaken anyone, but *you* may have forsaken Him. If that is true, come to the Light, dear ones. Redeem yourselves. Come to the Light.

The God of your Earth is a loving God. The God of your Universe is a loving God. He does not punish. Only you punish yourselves by your dark thoughts, your unhealthy living, by your addictions. It is always easier for those of lesser consciousness to blame someone else other than themselves. They play the victim well.

In the New World of spirituality and higher dimensions, there will be no victims. People will have love in their hearts. They will have peace. If there are arguments in relationships, people will know how to forgive each other so that eventually wars will be of the past. Will not that be a wonderful life to be born into where there will be no war but only harmony and balance between humanity and nature?

The birds will sing and come to you if you hold your hand out and will chatter to you and will peck seed from your hand. They may land on your head and play with your hair. You will be able to lie down in the meadows and not be afraid that a snake will come. You will lie down in the meadows and smell the fresh clover as the sun shines in the brilliant, clear sky.

The wind elemental will gently waft over you. You will be filled with peace and love. The animals that roam the forest will be your friends. They will come to you to be scratched behind their ears, or to drink some water that you may be providing them. It will be a glorious time, humanity.

So we will close now. We will close, Readers, with our blessings. In the following pages, we may separate and come one at a time in order to give you our messages. However, today we join with all of you. We blend with all of you. We gather you to us. We love you and bless you.

Greetings. *(10:15-10:35 AM)*

TABLE OF CONTENT

INTRODUCTION

Hello once again to this Channel and to our many Readers. It gives me the greatest pleasure to come back once again and announce that we are now ready to proceed with Book SEVEN. This Author wants to know the title already for it is easier for her to put the title on the pages at the beginning. However, we say that the title will remain un-clarified for now, for so much may change.

I Am Yeshua. I take great delight in coming this morning. We—a blend of us—gave you the *Foreword* yesterday and so today on this auspicious morning we will start this *Introduction*. It will be quite a few pages long so we will not be able to complete this in one sitting.

As we told you yesterday, the Earth is marching forward preparing herself for the hard days ahead. She knows that there will be many people making their transitions for various reasons. Some souls simply want out. Other souls have bodies that are worn out. Then there are those that are sticking it out, persevering, wanting to be a physical part of this great change the Earth is undergoing as she moves into her next dimension.

In the pages ahead, Readers, you will see that we have brought in several Presenters. Some have spoken before, while others have not. Each person will be giving you his or her wisdom that will pertain to the days ahead. Accept their wisdom as your knowledge and then let it become your wisdom. Always question what you read to see if it is true for you, for one must never accept anything that he or she has heard or read as the absolute truth, unless it is part of his/her knowledge and truth. Many times people wish validation so that they can become wiser in their own discernment. We are talking about *discernment.* That is difficult at times for people, for so much comes into play.

For America, this next year is centered upon the election, the election for a new president, a new leader for America. Amazingly enough there are those die-hards who still do not discern where the lies are, where the many non-truths are when their government speaks. Few true facts are given to the public at this time.

Your president rarely speaks from wisdom, for he is not the real person. Others have said this so I too will validate. **Your president is not real. He is a clone** and I will let you sit with that for a while. Many people in the world... (*I knew He was leading up to the topic of* clones.)

It was at this point that I asked for a side-bar, as I really did not want to discuss clones *in my book. It was then that I lost contact with Yeshua. I think he just left for there was only silence. We have been taught that one must never force a transmission for most likely it is no longer the Master speaking but one's ego-personality, or worse yet, a dark energy has come in.*

So my lesson out of this is to transmit everything they are saying to me and then edit and censor or toss out later. Oh well, will see what he does Sunday, or if he even comes! (Well, he did come in and took up where I had interrupted him without any prompting on my part.)

(Lord, I apologize for disrupting the transmission yesterday and I ask for your forgiveness.) Oh, precious one, your apologies are accepted. What I would like to do this morning is to continue the Introduction and then I will come back and we will speak about what happened yesterday and the ensuing silence. Does that sound all right with you? (Yes, thank you.) All right, I would like to pick up where we left off yesterday where I was saying your president was a clone.

This may shock many of you Readers but at the same

time there are many of you who already know this. The act of *cloning* has gone on for many years, or we will say for millions of years on different planets and in different Universes. In many of those ancient times in those different worlds, cloning was used in order to keep a particular DNA from disappearing. No, the clones did not have souls, but that was not the clones' purpose. The purpose was to keep the creation from getting lost. If one had a brilliant mind one could clone that person and keep that brilliant mind—keep the DNA from becoming contaminated.

I know this goes against every grain in most people's bodies, for they think of cloning as being lesser than being created from God. And it is! However, it is used throughout the worlds. Earth is not the only world that does this. Cloning has a higher sense and a higher value under different circumstances in different worlds.

Cloning on Earth, however, is not of the higher order. It is merely to perpetuate what the dark forces have created. The Illuminati clone in order to keep their kind going as an exact replica. It fools many people who do not carry much discernment. That is what is going on with your government. Many officials in your government are clones. They are not the true self because the true self may be on life-support systems or they could even be dead. I will not go into this further. This Author has made her wishes known that she does not want this book to be one of describing the dark energies, but rather to be an uplifting book. So much written can be of the dark, you see, and there are other authors out there who do this. It is their purpose.

However, it is not our purpose. We wish to enlighten you Readers as to what is going on in the spiritual world. Unfortunately, cloning is a part of the lesser consciousness that resides on Earth at this time. Yet all of that will be a thing of the past, for as the Earth raises her frequencies—her vibrations—that lower thinking to clone someone just to keep perpetuating the dark energies will no longer be able to be sustained! The energy is too low. The vibration is too low.

As one advances in the dimensions, one vibrates more and more rapidly. We Masters vibrate at a very high frequency of 500 or more. The average person is doing well to get up to 200. Therefore, you see the controversy here. Cloning is not at a high vibration on Earth, for there is no soul in the clone. It is the soul that permeates the body. It is the soul that brings in the Light, brings in the love which increases the vibration. Clones are not able to do this in this world.

As we have said, in other worlds the vibration is higher and the cloning then is at a higher frequency. However, for Earth it is not so; for Earth it is not correct. It is not from God. Test-tube babies are not from God. Test-tube animals are in the experimentation stage. Man has a history on Earth of reaching into the Universal Mind and bringing back information that humanity is not ready to receive. That is what happened with the atomic and the hydrogen bombs. Humanity is not ready for that type of energy. They use it in a negative way. The scientific information about cloning is in the same category. Humanity at this time is not ready for that information, for it is only used to control people on Earth. It is usury and it is not correct. However, we shall say no more about this in the Introduction since that is not meant to be the main focus of this book.

There is a well-known Soul standing in the wings waiting to usher in this book. This great Being that is waiting to speak is known to most of you, if not all. I will step back now and come back at a later time. (*Thank you, Yeshua.*) You are welcome.

Good morning, precious Readers, it is so good to be back with you once again. **I Am Lady Nada** and I do enjoy conversing with you. If there are some of you who do not know me, I am your Lord Yeshua/Sananda's Consort, his

Twin Ray in every aspect. Or you could say, *where he goest, I goest too.! (Smiles.)*

Now what do we have in store for you for this book? Each of our books refers to those ancient Biblical times, but they are more in passing reference now. It is no longer the focus of our books. Therefore, for you Readers who wish to be brought up to date, go back to the fourth book, *Realities of the Crucifixion;* or go to the fifth book, *Messages from the Heavenly Hosts;* or the sixth book, *Your Space Brothers and Sisters Greet You!* And now we have this seventh one with the title pending.

In those ancient times, the Biblical era times that you refer to as the *Jesus* era, I will say that the name *Jesus* was the Greek translation of *Yeshua.* That is what we called him, *Yeshua.* My body at that time was *Mary Magdalene.* So many of you have read the distorted writings about our relationship. Consequently, I will say very quickly and succinctly that Yeshua and Mary Magdalene were married and had several children. There were no illegitimate children. I was never married to anyone else, although an author has linked me to John the Baptist. That is not true. Another author has linked me to Judas and that is not true.

I was linked only to Yeshua, who in actuality was the Lord Sananda and your God, Christ Michael. It was His body that He created so that He could walk your Earth and know what it was like for just an hour or so at a time to be human. That was the reason. He wanted to experience everything. In that way, you see, Yeshua and I as Mary Magdalene married and had children and traveled and experienced spiritual work and Initiations—what you would call a *New Age way of being.*

We were all of that. We were Essenes. We taught and we prayed to God. We played. To the best of our ability we helped people; we healed people. Not much is written, if any, about my healings. However, many times when Yeshua was healing someone, I too was at his side, holding the energy.

INTRODUCTION

We did not focus on the illness, you see. We focused only on the wellness that we saw. We saw the soul, and we would bring the souls closer into their body. We saw the beautiful Light then in the body, and we would bring more energy and bring more Light into that ill person. The illness or disease then could not live in that higher vibration. Thereby, it dissipated. The darkness of illness changed into the light of health and the person was healed. We were a team. We did this together or separately. Since there was such a distinction between males and females, patriarch and matriarch, many times Yeshua would be healing men and I would be healing the women. Together many times we would be healing children.

So many times in Christianity there is a healing service. This is what Yeshua and I did. We were a healing team together. Did we have our disagreements? Of course we did. We were in a relationship *(chuckles)* and in all relationships there are disagreements, but we were able to laugh and rise above them. At one time there was a longer time of separation—a separation because we did not agree on a particular action. Therefore, we separated in order to gain a different perspective and then we came back together stronger than ever.

Marriages in those ancient times were different than they are now.   The commitments were similar, but there was no court or lawyers or judges to tell you what to do. People used their Rabbis or spiritual leaders to counsel them. When we were with the Essenes, Anna, the grandmother of Yeshua, was a great counselor, as she is to this day. Today people place their spiritual counselors in boxes—religious boxes.

The Mother Mary is still trying to get out of that box that the Catholics have put her into. Of course when I say she is *trying*, she has long left that idea and never did agree with it. The religious leaders are the ones who placed her into that box. The Catholics owned her. Any time someone has a picture of Mother Mary or has a piece of jewelry of the

INTRODUCTION

Mother holding a Babe, the person wearing it is immediately thought to be Catholic. Even during modern Crusades, one rarely hears the Mother being mentioned. And never Lady Nada (*smiles*).

If I as Mary Magdalene am ever mentioned, it is always as the *sinner,* the one tearing over Yeshua's feet and wiping his feet with my hair. When the church decided to make up its own stories, it had some scribes and priests who were quite dramatic with their own ideas. Since they had to be celibate, they were determined to make me a *fallen woman (chuckles)*. Now that we have distanced ourselves from the drama, we don't know whether to laugh or to cry. Some of it is so silly, while some of it is so extraordinarily evil—yes, evil.

How could the minds of men become so dark with their own puffed-up egos wanting power and wanting to control? They were so puffed up that they were willing to snuff out the life of anyone who dared disagree with them, especially someone who drew crowds to him like Yeshua did. Remember, there were no televisions, radios, or newspapers. Yet sometimes news by word-of-mouth went just as swiftly—not always accurately—but swiftly.

When there were momentous occasions when they knew that Yeshua was going to speak, crowds would quickly gather. At first he would climb onto a little hill so that he could be seen and his voice would carry. When that became too crowded, he would climb to a higher spot or stand in a boat. But then people started to come too close. They pulled on his garments, wanting to touch him. It became too much, for he felt their emotions. You know, no matter how much Light you carry, when people of lesser consciousness are pressing on you, it becomes a juggling act on how to stay balanced. As that energy would sweep over him, it would be a struggle for him to keep balanced.

He turned to his family, his mother, cousin-sister, brothers and me. Some of the best times would be when we would be invited into an enclosed garden where the crowds could be kept outside of the walls and where there was peace inside the courtyard and among the trees. That was wonderful for we could revitalize ourselves; sit in the shade and sip a cup of cool water; nibble on fruit, nuts, and dried figs, and rest our weary bones. We would bathe and take turns massaging each other's tired calves and feet.

Those were turbulent times, Readers. It came to a head when they wanted to crucify him! I could not be with him when he was being condemned, for there would be no women allowed in those areas. I could only peer through the small openings in the walls. My heart would cry out in pain for his pain that he was suffering. It got to the point where we knew that we must leave the country, for his accusers were bent on killing him. I will not go into any more detail. It is pretty much said in our Book FOUR. But we left. We left the country and traveled to India.

Presently, we are working diligently with people on Earth. We are watching America as she struggles with electing a new president and a new government. The different candidates who are running have gotten into bickering back and forth in the Democratic party. In the Republican party the candidate is just sitting by, watching the bickering across the aisle.

There is still a possibility that an Independent candidate may enter the ring. He is standing by and we are watching him. The next president will be blessed by God. He cannot do it for you, America, for God must let you have your free will. However, He can bless the candidate of your choice. Be aware that the Illuminati hangs over the heads of the people in the Democratic party as well as the people in the Republican party. Choose wisely, for if you do not, you will get four more years of the same.

The new president must have the expertise to embrace the New World, to embrace change, to embrace Light and not come from greed and love of power and money. While there is power in all high positions—it is an energy source—that power resides in all people in those high positions and can lead them into great negativity. One needs to know how to work with power-energy and not use it in destructive ways. The war ought never to have happened. The next president will withdraw those troops.

I have spoken quite a bit of the past and some of the present, as I am wont to do. Whether this introduces the book or not, I do not know, but this is what I felt I wanted to say this morning. I will close now, but we are not finished. Humanity, choose well, for you are choosing your future! Choose well.

I AM Lady Master Nada, the Consort of Lord Sananda. Adieu. *(Thank you, Lady, thank you.)* You are welcome, dearest one; you are welcome.

All right dear one, let us have our little side-bar here as to what went on yesterday. (Yes, again I apologize and ask you to forgive me for just stopping the transmission cold. There is a part of me that feels that so much has been written on clones *that I did not want to bring it up in my book as though I am plagiarizing. I was coming from that.) We understand, dear one, and you had time to figure how it impacted the energy. (Yes.) You were correct.*

It did stop us and I also left because I could not become a part of that energy. (Yes.) It was controlling; it was a controlling energy, you see. (Yes, I did recognize that.) But you did recognize it and that was the main thing. You were quite right that the correct way to do this is to let it roll—just like a movie screen. Let it roll on and then you and Heather can do all the editing you wish with it afterwards.

So dear one, are you finished with all of that?(Yes, but I still do not have a clear idea what this book will be about.) Neither do we (chuckles). We leave it up to the Presenters who come in. They will be speaking mostly about present times, but as you see my dear Nada wanted to bring Readers up to date. (Yes, I can see how new Readers need to have this information of the Biblical era.) In each book we will say that there was no crucifixion. In that way the word goes out. (Yes.)

Now dear one, we will set this up like we did the last time. It gives you more time to transcribe without undue stress. We will come every other day. This is not meant to be an academic exercise, but one of joy. And we recognize that there may be times you will have family obligations and will wish to not sit during those times. (Yes, thank you. It does give me great joy. I am so thankful you came today after I blew it yesterday.) But dear one is this not a learning for you (chuckling)? (Yes, it truly is. Just as my ego says, oh, boy I have this under control and then I blow it!) Laughingly, but that is how lessons are learned. We did not really leave you, you know. We just sort of side-stepped the energy. (Yes, I was controlling it, that's for sure. Thank you, Lord.) You are welcome, our dearest one.

You know you are close to our heart for Eternity. Did you hear that? (Yes.) You are a part of us for Eternity. We will take our leave for now, but know I am always with you. I hear you; I feel you; I see you. Whenever you are in real need, I am with you at that moment when you think of me, although I am always with you all the time anyway, but you do not know that. Saint Germain is also here. We are with you always. (Thank you, Lords, thank you.)

All right my dear, that's it for today. Greetings with love. (Hmmm, thank you.) 10:15AM

Good morning our precious ones, this Channel and our precious Readers. It is I, **Yeshua***. With me are Saint Germain and Ashtar. We are becoming quite the triplets. We will take up where we left off, for we are still writing the Introduction of this book.*

INTRODUCTION

This morning my dear Brother Saint Germain is going to speak with you for a while. He has a great following throughout the world, and it gives us the greatest pleasure to have him consent to speak within the pages of this book. I will step aside now and let him begin.

Good morning everyone, I am the Soul you know as **Saint Germain**, although I have come many times with different names. For those of you who may not know, I was **Father Joseph**, the father of our great Brother and Lord Yeshua/Sananda. It was the greatest privilege that God had given me—the assignment to be the parent of His body that He had prepared.

Readers, God wears many hats and He was wearing the hat of Christ Michael when He brought sweet Mary and me together, along with Archangel Gabriel. We formed the body that the world has called *Jesus,* but that is the Greek translation. We wish people who speak of that great person to refer to him as *Yeshua.*

For the Introduction of this book, each of us Presenters is going to present a particular theme so that the book will be a compilation of our thoughts, teachings, and our love. I come through many people, giving many messages. Each message is not all that different but the energy, you see, is different because I come through a different Channel.

This particular Channel and I have great history together. She has been with me for many lifetimes, many lifetimes on Earth anyway. She has not had that many on Earth—53-54. She is known in other worlds, not by her present name, but by other names.

My theme throughout this book has to do with your allowing yourself to receive. *Allowing* is an interesting energy. Everything is energy. When a person allows something, then there is an agreement to accept a viewpoint, or to receive information. People who control a great deal struggle with the allowing energy, for that allowing energy carries no control. It is merely a giving energy.

When you give something, are you not allowing that information or that product to be received? So many times people who have a hard time receiving are not allowing that gift to be given to them. They are not allowing that energy to come toward them, to come forth. It is a concept that is difficult for people to understand sometimes, for *allowing* and *receiving* can be part of the same coin.

This Channel allows me to speak to her telepathically. In doing that, she is receiving my words. It is very simple. Now *allowing* becomes more difficult when another person is giving forth his/her information and maybe someone else does not agree with i*t.* You do not have to agree with everything, but you do need to have the *allowing energy* in place. Allow the person to say whatever he or she wishes to say and then you will either accept it or you will not receive it yourself. But you have allowed the other one to speak his or her piece—one's wisdom.

Do you have a problem in receiving? If you have a problem in receiving, then you have a problem in allowing others to give to you, whatever that may be. It may be as simple as receiving an apple, or as simple as a book, or as simple as a prayer, or as simple as a gift of money. Do you receive it well? It may be as simple as someone wishing to pay for your meal. How many of you say, *oh no, that is all right?* You are not allowing that person to give to you. Those are some of the examples that I can think of at this time in order for you to grasp the meaning—allowing, receiving are parts of the same coin.

Let us dig deeper with that. We have heard so many times, *oh I wish the Masters would speak to me!* We are saying, are you allowing us to do so? In other words, how many times have we come to you and you would not receive us? You would not receive us because you already had it set up as

24

to how we were and what we were to say—how we would approach you.

Therefore, in that way you did not allow us to be who we are and thereby, you did not receive us. Consequently, you received no messages. One must look at it in depth for it can be tricky. *Allowing* and *receiving* pretty much permeate everything a person does in his or her world. Allow the information that the different Presenters will give you in this book to come to you in undiluted form. Then it is your discernment as to whether you wish to make it your wisdom or not. But allow the knowledge to come forth so that you can turn it into your wisdom.

It gives us great joy to speak to you, Humanity. We are so delighted when people receive us and allow us to be who we are. We have heard the remarks that sometimes we are exuberant in our *endearments* or in our endearing terms. We say, *precious*; we say, *dearest ones*; we say, *we love you (much chuckling)*. Some people cannot receive that; they cannot allow us to be that way. They think of that as being too *gooey* instead of allowing us our energy. You see those endearments carry a great deal of love. If you allow those to come in and allow us to be that way and to let those terms come in, the energy that you will be receiving will be full of love.

Even this Channel sometimes says, *can't we calm down all of those endearing terms a bit?* She tries to control that once in a while. Does it work? NO *(chuckles)*. She is stuck with it and maybe this will also help her to know that each time we use an endearment it is full of love for not only her, but for all of you.

So with that I think I will use a very gooey closing sentence and say, allow me, precious ones, allow me, dearest ones, to come into your heart with my deepest love for you.

I AM Saint Germain *(still chuckling)*

INTRODUCTION

(Oh, Saint Germain, you got me! Oh, dear, you got me, breaking out laughing.) I did, didn't I? And it was such fun. Thank you for allowing that, thank you. *(And I have received it, still in merriment.)* Greetings, dear one.

Good morning, Readers and to our precious Channel. We are affectionately known as the Gang to this Channel, as in the song, "the Gang's all here." We are continuing this book and we have just a few more Presenters to speak before we start the chapters. So without further words from me, let the next person come forth and have his segment. (All right).

Hello to our Readers and to this Channel. This is **Ashtar of the Ashtar Command.** *(Hello Ashtar!)* Good morning to all of you. It is quite a glorious, sunny morning in Arizona. So many people are having tornadoes and floods, but when we come to Arizona it is always sunny and there is a slight breeze blowing. It is delightful.

We are writing the seventh book and it gives us such joy to be a part of this. You see, Readers, even though there are thousands and even millions of people who channel the Masters, there are still billions of people who do not! Therefore, it gives us great pleasure when we can come forth to an individual who carries a higher frequency so that she/he can actually communicate with us. We are so delighted—so delighted. Each time I come I think, *now OK, what can I say that I have not said to all the other thousand of channels that I come through?* No matter what I say, it will have a different tone simply because it **is** a different Channel.

This Channel received in the mail a little four page newsletter put out by *Share International (The Emergence Vol.XXVI No.2 March 2008. In it Benjamin Crème channels Lord Maitreya and validates what many people question about seeing Him in various disguises.)* On the back of the newsletter is a picture of one of the mother ships from Mars and the person is asking for validation as to the truth. It was a triangular shape and each side was approximately

300 feet long, which the article said is the size of a football field. There it was in the sky—so big that you could spot it. (*Benjamin Creme's Master confirms that the ship was from Mars.*) These happenings are occurring throughout your world. It is the announcement of things to come. I am of the Ashtar Command, but there are many Commands, and we are all of the Federation of Light. All of these Commands have joined the Federation of Light.

Now do all the Beings/Souls look like Earthlings? NO. However, all are striving for a higher consciousness in order to get in touch with that spiritual aspect of themselves.

This Channel likes to watch on TV the different episodes of the star ships. Right now she is watching the *Battleship Galactica* and finding it intriguing. The actors all go charging off in their ships and are *jumping* the dimensions. Much of that is true. Those action-words were channeled, you see. However, the actors' ships are not as beautiful as ours. Those TV ships are metallic, more of a machine, where ours are energies of Light and everything is softer. Everything is quieter. There is not the tension and drama as are portrayed in the TV dramas.

However, those TV shows would not even be presented if there were not an interest in them. Every time there is an interest, there is a reason. It is a wake-up call. It means we are coming. We wrote the previous book, *Your Space Brothers and Sisters Greet You!* We told you of the wonderful things that will come to you if you will allow us to land. People would do well to study Saint Germain's teaching on *allowing*, for people must allow us to be who we are. Your government would like nothing better than to make us prisoners of war— to instill fear in the mind of the public. However, there is nothing to fear, as we have said. We are love and we come with love and our ships are of love and Light.

Much is going on in your world these days. I will focus on America at this time. She is struggling. She is struggling with her economy. It is all part of that old adage, *energy must reach rock-bottom before it can come back up into the Light.* The banking situation is going through immense changes. The media is not allowed to tell all. Some of the reporters of the economy like to say, *it's a contraction. It is not a recession until you have had two months of contraction in a row.* We say, horse putty! It's a recession. Now will there be a depression? Not if you remove the present government and bring in new life.

We heard an uplifting commentary yesterday that if the Democratic Party fights against each other to the point where they are tearing each other apart, there will be a new candidate by the name of Al Gore who steps in. There are many people who do not like him for various reasons known only to themselves. We say of all the candidates, he's the one who knows how to lead, having been a vice president. He knows national diplomacy, having been a vice president; he knows the importance of maintaining the health of the planet. (*Al Gore did not step forth.*)

Some people say that there is no global warming. But he (*Gore*) does grasp the situation well and has earned a Nobel Prize. Which one of all those candidates, America, has **his** credentials? There were a few good men running, but they have received little attention and have either dropped out or are still struggling on. The one with the most support and energy at this time is the one who was supposed to be president before it was stolen by George W. Bush. That is common knowledge. The Supreme Court played into that nicely as did the Florida legislative branch. Why would it not when the Bush brother was the governor?

Pay attention to your choices, dear ones. There has to be a change made in the public's thinking, in their consciousness. Yes, they have free will, but if you have a higher frequency and a higher vibration, you will not make a choice for war. You will not make the choice for greed like the oil companies

INTRODUCTION

and their billions of dollars of profit, letting America strangle herself on the high prices for fuel.

This is unthinkable to our mind, for it is not taking into consideration all of the people, but only the very few of the top echelon. The common man or woman would like to travel to a state park to see the wonders of the geyser waters spewing out of the Earth. Or they would like to drive to the Grand Canyon. Yet with the price of gasoline, those on the lower economic rung of the ladder cannot afford to go sight seeing.

Yes, they can make peanut butter sandwiches to bring along, but they cannot afford to journey far. It is similar to the time of the 60-70's when you had the Volkswagen buses and you could pull off along the side of the road and make your sandwiches and sleep in the bus—that's when gasoline was cheap.

This will all change, dear ones. Keep your faith and raise **your** vibrations. Do not get caught up in the negativity of the world. There is that expression—I love using the different expressions of Earthlings—*keep your own nose clean and do not worry about someone else's.*

It is time, America, for a wake-up call. Allow us to come; allow us to land; allow us to reach out our hand to you; allow us to give you our love; allow us to give you our technology; allow us to give you the new medical modalities, what some people would say is *alternative medicine.* Allow us to show you how you can heal with Light and sound. It will come, but it will come sooner if you will raise your vibrations and raise your consciousness and fill your heart with love.

We are coming, dear ones. There is that saying *you cannot stop progress* and that is true. As the Earth marches on toward 2012, you cannot stop progress. That then means that all of that dark, non-complying energy, all the greed and lies must come forward to be transmuted into Light. Let go of

29

those dark, sexual games, many of which are played in your government. Let go of the belief that one religion is better than another. Let go of the damning of the homosexuals. You have no idea; you do not know what you are talking about. Those are life choices and life-games that their souls have set up in order to learn very intricate lessons.

There is a great deal of autism among children these days. It is said that it is from the inoculations, the vaccines possibly. That could be the catalyst, but unless there was a problem in the birth of the child, the child is autistic because of the soul's choice. The soul wishes to experience that. Maybe in the next lifetime that soul will be a teacher of autistic children or will be in the medical field working with autism. Consequently, you see that each generation has a reason for what happens, whether it is the health issues of children, or the schooling, or parenting, these are soul choices—the free will gone rampant. All of this will calm down. Many of those are three dimensional people, coming into the fourth dimension, or fourth dimensional people coming into the fifth, although there are fewer of those at this time. These conditions will be transmuted, people, and love and peace shall reign upon the Earth once more.

I Am Ashtar of the Ashtar Federation of Light ships and I greet you.

(*Thank you, Ashtar.*) *Y*ou are welcome and we are coming! (Yes.)

All right, dear one, that ought to do it for today. (Thank you.)

Dear Readers and to this Channel, we are back once again, The Gang, as you know us by now. We have come to finish up the Introduction of this book and to bring some closure to all that we have been saying.

INTRODUCTION

Sometimes we get carried away with all that is going on on Earth. Consequently, we may have a tendency to rattle on which may seem like it has no purpose for you. However, understand that even though it seems as if we are rattling on, we are conscious of what we are saying—just as you need to be. You need to control your thoughts. This Channel has been sitting for a half hour waiting for us, and when her thoughts went hither and yon, she would bring them back and concentrate more on us. As she sat contemplating in appreciation for what she calls this privilege of writing a book, we then descended.

Watch your thoughts, dear ones; it is extremely important these last days leading to 2012, for if those thoughts of yours are centered on peace, love, and Light, that is what will help Mother Earth. That is what will bring about the peace that you all dream of having.

Now for our last Presenter, I wish to bring in a woman so that we will always maintain balance between the masculine and feminine energies or principles, you may say. This Channel is balanced in her own energies to the point that many times people on the Internet cannot tell whether she is male or female because of the energies of her names.

She has amusing little dream symbols that when she is coming from her masculine energies her dream shows her sprouting whiskers on her face, much to her perturbed feminine side (chuckles). However, it is rather humorous to us. Now let us step aside and let this last Presenter come forward.

Good morning to all of you precious children. **I AM** the **Divine Mother** and it gives me the greatest pleasure to come forth. As this Channel is sitting here in the alcove of her bedroom where she channels, there is a large lemon tree outside of her window and the morning doves build their nests in this tree. There is much cooing and fluttering of wings as they fly in and out. In other bushes and trees

INTRODUCTION

the birds are trilling, singing their songs. This Channel is playing beautiful harp music by Peter (*The Angels' Gift, a CD by Peter Sterling*). It all sets the scene, so to speak—a scene of serenity and peace.

When we enter close as we do, we sense the peace that resides in her heart and all around her. She has been told by Saint Germain that peace emanates from her so that by sitting in her presence one feels peaceful. One is calmed by her energy. This is the same energy that she brought forward from those Biblical times when she used to sit with your Master and her presence calmed those energies that would rage through him. She is known throughout the Universes, but she is not aware of this.

Many times we have come to her, for she too struggles at times—you know, family issues of health of some kind. As the people are healed, her energy calms down and she can regain her peace once again.

Would it not be wonderful, Readers, if all of you could tap into that energy band? It is an energy band, you know. It is energy, dear ones. Everything is energy. Peace is energy. Tap into that energy, dear ones. Bring peace into your lives. You have heard, I'm sure, where there must be peace in your heart before you can bring peace to others and the world.

When you are in your still time, remember to be in your heart, be in your Light and love, and to be sure to tap into those bands of energy so that you can then give them to Mother Earth. Give them out to your government, America, for it needs much peace.

This book will hold many teachings from the different Masters. Generally speaking, we have pretty much covered what needs to be said as far as those Biblical eras are concerned. We do not need to rehash that anymore, for you see, one of the tasks that your souls are doing is bringing your

INTRODUCTION

pasts forward, transmuting those dark, past lives—gleaning the wisdom from them and then letting them go.

Many of you have had very dark lives that your souls have chosen for the learning experience, you see. If you will look at history in a chronological way, you can see where souls would incarnate at those specific times, simply for the learning experience. Therefore, if you are reading about a Biblical era, know that you have had a lifetime in that era.

People who read about the Inquisition have had a lifetime in that particular time period. If you condemned someone in the Inquisition, you came back in a subsequent lifetime and were condemned yourself. It always plays back and forth.

How about in America in those pioneer days with the people crossing the prairies in those covered wagons—most uncomfortably? Those were your past lives. There was much to learn then in those frontier towns.

You had lives as American Indians. You fought for your survival. Then you had reverse lives fighting against the Indians' survival. Therefore, you did not come in just once, but several times in order to experience a particular period in history.

Now that is not to be any longer, those lives are to be transmuted. You are to look carefully as to why you chose those lives. What was it that you wanted to learn? Then you are to ponder on that and to glean the wisdom of that truth and whether you have incorporated it into your present life. Are you walking your talk after you have learned it? Or, are you rehashing the same thing over and over and over? As Lady Nada said in one of our books, *why do you keep choosing such cruel lifetimes repeatedly?* Once or twice is enough, but over and over is not necessary.

Look at how dark the Crusades were in those ancient times. Men rode out under the guise of seeking the Holy Grail. What folly! Those knights ended up plundering,

33

INTRODUCTION

killing, and raping, all in the name of God. God did not sanction any of that! That was man's free will. That was the church saying, *go out and kill the heretics; go out and kill the mothers and wives of the heretics for we do not want any more of those evil children being born.* It was such a near-sighted perspective.

If you have progressed in your consciousness, and most of you reading these books have, know that all of those dark lives were orchestrated by the dark energies—many of what you would call the Reptilians. Not all Reptilians are dark, however. Many are seeking to know the spiritual path. But back in those terrible, dark, historic times, the Reptilian forces carried little to none of the Light and spirituality. All they wanted was the power. As you have learned, power is also an energy force that can be used with the greatest negativity.

As you move closer to 2012, you are bringing many of those past lives forward. Some people have hundreds of past lives on this planet. Some have very few, for they come from other planets, as this Channel does. However, she experienced those dark eras for she needed to know about them firsthand. And yes, she did repeat some of them just like all of you have done.

Therefore, your task in this lifetime you have chosen is to bring those past lives forward and glean the wisdom from them and then let them go. Do not glamorize them; do not dramatize them; and do not yearn for them. That is old energy, third dimension for sure and some were even second dimension. You do not want that old energy. Bring it up into present time. Bring your energy into the fifth dimension if you possibly can.

Each time you move up a dimension you vibrate at a higher frequency. Therefore, those dark energies cannot live with you for their vibrations are too low. Many of the illnesses that you suffer from have the lower frequencies, as you have

INTRODUCTION

been told. Consequently, as you raise your vibration, you will not suffer those illnesses anymore.

You see a predominance of cancer remissions these days. That is because the person has raised his or her vibration and the cancer cannot continue to live. Some of you of the Newer Age have had cancer or have family members and friends who have cancer and perhaps you have heard of the program that this Author will tell you about at the end of this segment.

It is a program where you send your picture to this company. Your energy is on the picture. Your frequencies are in the picture. The picture is run through a computer daily. The computer erases the frequencies of cancer and many, many other conditions. You would need to get in touch with the company to learn more about it.

While this Channel does not have cancer, she believes whole heartedly in this alternative medical field and has been a participant in this program for several years. We recommend it highly.

It is time, Readers. It is time to transmute what you have in your knapsack. In one of our books we told about souls who bring in their karmic baggage in their knapsack. It is time to transmute all of that. Change your thoughts to the higher thoughts. Reside in the higher frequencies. Be full of love and peace. The more love you have the more Light you will carry, for they are of the same coin. It is time. This is all I wish to say for this morning. We know who you are; we know who you are, dear Lightworkers.

I AM Mary known to you as the Divine Mother.

(*Thank you Mother Mary.*) You are welcome, child.

(*Author's note: Here is the information that the Mother asked me to make available to you. I receive no compensation for this. If you will come from the belief that all is energy*

INTRODUCTION

(E=MC2) and thereby our pictures carry our frequencies, then it becomes plausible that these frequencies can be altered through a computer program. Evan Slawson is the computer genius who partnered with Dr. Stephen Lewis to create the AIM program. Their book, **Sanctuary,** *available at most libraries and book stores, describes their processes of arriving at the* **AIM program,** *which alters over 250 unhealthy conditions—cancer, AIDS, MS, Autism, etcetera— from which humanity suffers. The company's address is:*

EMC2 2349-A Renaissance Drive, Las Vegas, NV 89119 Phone # 702-944-1801

Some people groan over the expense. I think of it as my health-insurance policy. There are several payment plans and Family and Pet plans, also.)

Turn the page now and let us continue the book with Chapter 1 for you.

CHAPTER 1- GENEROSITY

Good morning once again to our Readers and to our precious Channel who is willing to take this project on— to take it on on our behalf for there are observations and teachings and belief systems that we wish to convey to you. What better way to do it than through channeling which then becomes a book? While this Channel sits here in appreciation for our doing this with her, we too are in deep appreciation for the service that she provides us.

I AM Yeshua and I come this morning to start our Chapter 1. We have finished our long *Introduction,* and as my Lady Nada said, she was not sure if (*her segment*) was an *Introduction* or not. Anyway, she still said her piece (*chuckles),* as many of the Presenters did.

This seventh book does not have a particular theme as the previous one did on the spaceships. We thought we would address different questions that we see humanity pondering. We have repeated the information many times so that the new Readers would get caught up. Also, sometimes a person needs to read or hear a particular concept repeatedly before it sinks in, for knowledge that may not always be compatible with your own must go through many layers of belief systems

You have a choice, you see; you have a choice whether to change. We would warn you; always be willing to change, for nothing is static. Nothing stays static. Information changes. If you have made it into belief systems, most likely they need changing, dear hearts.

What I am going to talk about this morning can be up-lifting for some, for it validates what they already know, or it can be a downer for others. We are talking about one's giving—generosity. I would like to title this chapter, *GENEROSITY.*

There is usually a concept in people's minds about *generosity.* To them it means that someone has given away a certain amount of money. However, there are many levels of generosity. There is generosity of Spirit. There is generosity of camaraderie; there is generosity in giving; there is generosity in receiving. Generosity is not just giving money.

If you were driving down the street and saw a homeless person sitting on a bench with his/or her bags in a shopping cart, would it not be generosity of Nature to stop your car and approach the person and hand him/her a bottle of water, or sandwich, or a piece of fruit? People are so afraid now to approach the homeless. *Oh, don't give that person money; he or she will just go buy liquor with it; or he or she will go buy drugs with it and not food.* Sometimes this is true.

However, dear Readers, what I want to impress upon you is that that homeless person sitting on that bench could very well be a Master in disguise. That Master would be giving people a chance to be generous—giving them an opportunity to broaden their hearts and to awaken their generosity.

Sometimes people become complacent and they are warned so much not to give to the people begging on the streets. We say to recognize the God in that person. Recognize that that person could have been you in a past life; or that person could really be in need.

Do not approach the homeless with a negative attitude. Approach the homeless with a giving heart. If you fear that the person might be addicted to drugs or alcohol (and alcohol is a drug), give something that will bring comfort. Bring a blanket; bring a small pillow; bring food that will not spoil—a large salami would last a long time and would provide needed protein. The added fat would provide warmth for the body. If you think about it, there are all kinds of

GENEROSITY

things that you could give that would open and re-awaken this generosity that you carry.

How many times have people just rolled their windows up and driven on by? Yes, we recognize that some of the people who beg at a curbside or at stop signs are just out to make money. They have found a way to survive, but they are still a part of you. We are all one in this Universe. They are a part of you.

When you give to that person, are you not giving to yourself? How much you give to someone in need is how much will be returned to you. You have heard this repeatedly—*like measure. What you give, you will receive.* In this term or concept of generosity, it takes a generous soul to survive in today's world.

You may have thought generosity was more of a personality trait, but it is not. Generosity is a soul trait. The soul brings this in, for souls are learning also. You are not just given attributes. You earn them and they become a part of you. This is a soul attribute of generosity.

When you know it is the soul's makeup, does that not make it easier for you to approach another soul in need— one soul to another? You do not have to believe what that personality is saying to you while begging, for you know there could be a lie in there. However, there also could be a truth.

Look at how the person is dressed or washed. These are hints, but not always. The public has been brain-washed. *Do not give to the unkempt beggar for he or she may go home, shower, change clothes and go off to a bar looking as if he/ she has $50 in the pocket.*

Generosity, dear friends, is an attribute that is earned. Generosity comes in many forms, for it is soul led. Be generous in your thoughts towards other people; be generous

GENEROSITY

in your feelings and thoughts for Mother Earth and Nature; be generous in your giving.

If you wish to give to charities, spread it around. While some charities are worthwhile, others spend most of the money on staff. Research it and be sure that what you send, percentage-wise, goes for a good cause.

Is it important to give? YES. Again it is the giving; it is the giving. However, bear in mind that you must not over-give—*give yourself away.* Keep it in balance and do not over-give. Take care of yourself and then be generous in what you do with your time; be generous in sharing your Light, peace and joy with others. Take the time to visit those who are ailing; take the time to have lunch with a special friend. Do not be so caught up in your own life's story that you cannot reach out to others. Generosity comes in all descriptions, for it comes from the soul.

That is all I wish to say on this subject, so we will close for now.

I greet you, dear friends. Greetings.

CHAPTER 2- NADA'S THOUGHTS for HUMANITY

Hello to all of you Readers and to this Channel. We are back once again in order to proceed with our next chapter, Chapter 2. I will not be presenting that chapter but will be turning it over to a fellow Presenter right now.

Good morning to all of our Readers; it is so good to be with all of you once again. **I AM Lady Nada**. It is amusing that when I was coming in and this Channel was preparing to receive my name, she would keep getting *Yeshua*. She would then say, *no that's not right; he just left!* We are one, you know—my Twin Flame (*chuckles*). So it is Lady Nada, the Consort of your Jesus, the man we prefer to call Yeshua. That was his Hebrew name.

It is always such a loving time for us when we give you our thoughts and know that they are received so well. This Channel receives many e-mails praising the books and wanting more. Such remarks are truly songs to our heart. It is very gratifying, for it means you are awakening. Most of you are Masters and do not know it! (*Chuckles.*) Wake up to your Master hood, dear Readers.

In the past, and I am speaking of the times of Antiquity, not many of the Beings that came forth to experience those Biblical times were Masters. Of course the Holy Family were all Masters in disguise, we could say. The masses of people were still third dimensional, some were second dimensional and were not Masters.

Evolution is slow, but today many of the people who lived during that time are back once again. Therefore, there are many Masters walking your Earth. They are your Lightworkers and Lightweavers. Ashtar made the distinction in our last book that Lightweavers were weaving a product of some kind. The Lightworkers were walking and shedding their Light.

There is a dear soul named Beverly O'Connor. She is what we would call a fearless soul in that she will take off by herself and fly hither and yon literally into many foreign countries. As she is doing so, she is spreading her Light with every smile, every handshake, and every thank you. She learns different words in the foreign countries and loves meeting new people, tasting the foods, experiencing the emotions.

She is not always in agreement with the different countries she visits as in the suppression of women, for instance, but she carries the wisdom of that back and gives it forth to other people. She is a Lightweaver, you see, weaving those codes of Light as she travels. This Channel has nicked-named her *Johnny Appleseed,* for she is always dropping those Light codes with every step she takes.

As you have been told, this book has no particular theme, so it is up to us to bring in a specific teaching that we feel is important to recognize at this time. I am partial to different types of learning. I am partial to hearing and knowing about *Love*. I am partial to hearing about *Receiving*. I am partial to hearing and knowing about *Generosity* that my Flame has just spoken about. It is so important, for these little messages that we are giving you carry large amounts of energy that are imperative for you to bring into your own energy fields. We have talked so much about the benefits of your changing your belief systems in order to let new ideas in.

One of the areas we have not approached in this book is the great debates about stem-cell research, homosexuality, and various religious beliefs. Ought there to be contraceptives passed out in schools? Ought there to be abstinence versus a contraceptive? You can see where religions play into that, for it has long been taught in Catholicism that women not use

NADA'S THOUGHTS for HUMANITY

contraceptives but always be able and ready to receive the seed of their husband and co-create a baby.

In the olden days, we'll say, that probably was a true practice, especially in America when they were populating a new Nation. Also it was because the mortality rate among the little infants was so high that one had to keep on creating babies. If you lost one, you must have another one or you would have no names on your family tree. It was a necessity, but not from religions. It was a necessity for the population growth of the country.

However, now the whole world is over-populated. People now worry about that. In China there is a restriction on how many children you can have. In a way that is a good thing because China is over-populated. However, in an opposite way it has created evil of the worst kind because when there is a daughter born some families will kill that baby in order to bring in a son the next time. Families have killed many children, for if you are allowed only two children, they must be sons. If you happen to have only two daughters, they are not going to help you farm your lands and support you in your old age. Therefore, evil has come out of that edict. Where does one bring balance and how does one bring in the balance?

Does one just leave it up to God, as the saying goes—if He says you will become pregnant you will? If God says you won't, you won't? Now is that correct thinking? NO. I hope you hear that. NO, God does not decide how many children you will have, dear ones. Your body decides that; your genetic make-up decides that; your souls decide that— how many children are they going to bring in to transmute karma. There is so much involved with the soul agreements.

And there are families that do not want any children. They are afraid to bring children into this *terrible world*, as they put it. *Why would you bring children into a world that will be going through severe Earth changes,* they reason. But you see, evolution marches on. Karma itself will be different, for there will no longer be cause and effect particularly. When you are in the higher dimensions, most of your lifetimes will be of a more positive nature.

You will be kind to people. You will respect people; you will give to people. The darkness of energies coming to you will no longer happen. Therefore, souls will be playing out other games. Always keep in mind that evolution is slow. If you wish to end a particular addiction on that family-tree, like alcoholism, it could take several lifetimes. That is why you may keep returning in order to transmute that energy that the body carries. It is helping bodies to raise their vibratory rates.

Each time you have, shall we put it, conquered an addiction, you have raised the vibratory rate of your body. Now I know there is that saying that *you are addicted to chocolate* or what have you, but that is not the kind of addiction we are speaking of. We are speaking of those people who are heavily addicted to alcohol and other drugs, even sex.

Is not binging on food an addiction as well as crying out for either attention or comfort for the body? One must have a great deal of compassion for people who balloon to 300 pounds or more and the fact that many are house-bound because they no longer can get through the door, or into a car or airplane, However, you do not know what their life-agreements are. Was it to experience that terribly obese body, or it was to take that body and turn that addiction to food and wanting attention and transmute it and in that way clean up a family pattern, perhaps?

I am sure all of you have seen on TV where a terribly obese person would go on one of the regimented diets like Nutri-system, or Jenny Craig and lose tremendous amounts of weight. They have done so and love their new body. Sometimes they have been so overweight that when they do lose, they must have plastic surgery to remove pounds of hanging skin. These are experiences the soul has asked for— an addiction to binging and then sticking your finger down your throat in order to vomit it all out—the Bulimics—is a sad situation to behold, to be sure.

Is it not amazing how fragile the emotional body sometimes is? We have different bodies, as you have been told—etheric, spiritual, mental, emotional, and physical. It can be a difficult life for most people, for they are transmuting body addictions.

There has been much shown on TV concerning the homosexual community. Religions get into it and make their judgments, Do not judge them! I will make this statement and you can believe it or not: *every soul on the ladder of evolution has played that game of homosexuality.* They have chosen that lifetime. There is much learning in that.

There is learning of *tolerance*; there is the learning of *loving someone of the same gender* and being ostracized for it. There is learning in all aspects of a homosexual's life. It brings out the feminine principle in males. It brings out the masculine principle in females. Maybe those principles were underdeveloped in these people, so by choosing a lifetime of homosexuality, they learned to bring the masculine and feminine principles more into balance. Or, shall we say that they learn about them and then in the next lifetime they learn more about balancing those energies.

Now the idea of choosing a homosexual life will shock many of you, I know. But, dearest friends, think how old you are on a soul level. Goodness sakes! You are thousands and thousands and some even millions of years old. Of course you would play that game. Of course you would. Now do we of the Spiritual Hierarchy think that is a sin? Of course not! **Homosexuality is not a sin!** It is such a sad fact that your religions lay this damnation on homosexuals. There is not much more I will say about this, for we have spoken about it before, but your soul chooses this. Now we are aware that people many times choose this lifestyle; it is a *choice* during a lifetime. But that is a choice that the personality has made for various psychological reasons. However, a true homosexual is born into that. The soul has brought it in, whether male or female; the soul has chosen it as a learning experience. In the following lifetime, they may repeat it all again if they are still wanting to learn more facets of it; or they may start bringing the energy more into balance and end cycle with that way of being in the world.

When you are a homosexual male, the feminine intuition and the ability to decorate your environment may become stronger. A homosexual male may become a beautiful dancer, an artist, a couture designer, all those types of right brain activities—those creative abilities—become easier to acquire.

For the Lesbian, she is getting in touch with her masculine side—most likely working in a man's environment where she must use a great deal of male energy. You may find this in the workplace—maybe lawyers, any profession that uses that left-brain. Homosexuality, people, is a soul decision before you were born and/or it is a lifestyle decision stemming from psychological feelings that you have turned into problems.

Now what about stem-cell research, taking the stem cells from the umbilical cord of the fetus and using them in research in order to grow a limb, or to create something, or to heal a specific cancer, or to clone? Are we in agreement with that? That is a loaded question in that some of that could be correct and some of it would not.

When mothers have babies in these modern times, they are given a choice whether to allow the stem cells of the child to be saved for their use, perhaps, further on down the line. Maybe you may lose a limb and, with your stem cells, another limb could be made for you. It is all research. We are not in complete agreement, for again so much depends upon the pre-birth agreements.

On a more correct note, if the child or adult contracts a cancer—bone cancer—using some of his/her stem cells that have been frozen may help the person battle that condition.

The problem with any type of new genetically designed scientific procedure is whether one is interfering with Creation. There is no blanket response for this. There are so many mitigating circumstances that one cannot make a blanket statement to cover all of these factors. Many abuse this and do not use the stem cells in the correct way. There will be those who abuse it as in cloning.

Therefore, we cannot say definitively what is right or wrong for you. That is a soul's agreement. Use discernment, research, follow your inner guidance, even go to a *seer* of integrity to help you find the right answers for you. Just know that not everything you hear or see regarding scientific experiments or scientific new ideas can be pigeon-holed as a YES or NO.

I would like to name this chapter *Nada's Thoughts for Humanity.* Take the concepts in this chapter, Readers, as suggestions. It is hoped they will help you in your decisions, for everything you decide to do must stem from your own truth. Discovering your truth is the difficult part. Trust yourself; trust yourself.

Greetings to all of you, I AM Lady Nada.

CHAPTER 3- CHRIST MICHAEL

Good morning once again, precious ones, I AM Yeshua here with the Gang, and we are continuing our book. This Channel has been involved in spiritual work of the most important nature. She gave a beautiful presentation to a group of people and it was very well received. She is being honored by being asked to join Dhyana Markley's website. We are gratified. It is a good spot for her (www. AscendedMastersSpeak.com). Dhyana is one of our beloved messengers and chelas.

Now let us get to work on Chapter 3. As you may have noticed, we Masters are coming in with Teachings for this book. I would like you to name this book The Ultimate Experience: The Many Paths to God; The Teachings of the Masters of Light. *(Oh that's a beautiful title, thank you.) Yes, we thought so.*

As you know, the book would not be complete without a word from our Heavenly Father. Therefore, He is here, dearest Readers, to give forth His wisdom.

Good morning our dear children**, I AM** your **Father-Mother God,** and today I wear the Hat of My Aspect, **Christ Michael**. We spoke several times in the previous book, *Your Space Brothers and Sisters Greet You!* As Yeshua has said, I AM always a part of these most auspicious books. These books ring of much truth.

For you Readers who have yet to read *Realities of the Crucifixion,* or have read it and did not believe it, let Me validate that that is truth written. I Myself have collaborated in writing a book, *And Then God Said...Then I_Said...Then He Said...Volume One.* In this book were teachings that I wanted to give to humanity. I spoke with Suzanne Ward of

CHRIST MICHAEL

the *Matthew Messages*, I spoke with Celestial Blue Star of the Pleiades, and I spoke with David of Arcturus. The three of them and I created this wonderful book. (*Order the book at* www.bluestarspeaks.com).

Now I AM mentioning this in this Channel's book for when her books fan out to different people, they will read about (*My book*) and may wish to buy the new book that God has dictated to His messengers.

Many of you are from the old school. The old school dictates that you must have a go-between, to have someone to intercede for you with God. You must have an *Intercessor*, according to the Christian religion. Nothing could be further from the truth—nothing. I am available to you all, 24/7. I AM you! You look at your hands; that is a part of Me. You look at your Earth; that is a part of Me. Birds are singing outside this Channel's window. That is a part of Me. The Lemon tree that stands outside her window is a part of Me. I AM everywhere. I AM in each and every one of you.

Therefore, why would you need an Intercessor (*in order*) to touch Me when I already live in your heart and I AM already you? Why would you need anybody else to validate that you are Me? Is it not an interesting thought? As you know, your religions have gotten somewhat off-track. Their teachings have become distorted, and I will state that there is not one religion to this day that carries full truth! Hear this Readers—not one. That is a hard one for people to grasp, for they so desperately want to believe that everything that comes from the Torah has come from God; everything that is written in the Koran is from Allah; everything that is written in the Christian Bible is from God the Father and Jesus The Christ. Dear hearts of My heart nothing could be further from the truth.

Now in defense of those Books that I have just named, of course there is some truth in there, but it is not total truth! The rabbis spend many of what We would call *fruitless* hours

CHRIST MICHAEL

agonizing over how a word ought to be interpreted because that is what God meant. In My mind that is really a futile exercise; it is futile.

The true words were in the Commandments that I gave Moses. As you perhaps may have read on some of the Internet sites, your **Ascended Master Lord Kuthumi was Moses.** As he has written and I will say, I gave him 99 Commandments, not all of which have been passed on to humanity.

For those of you who may wish to know more about this, you may contact Michelle Ellof *(Johannesburg, South Africa)*, for she does a magnificent job of opening her vehicle so that Lord Kuthumi can step into her and give forth his truths. (www.enquiries@thelightweaver.org.)

One of the reasons We enjoy writing these books is because We have taken it upon ourselves to be a resource for you. In our books We guide you to different Internet sites; We guide you to different publications so that you might have another avenue in order to delve into the mysteries of life.

One of My sweetest moments—many of My sweetest moments—is when I am conversing with that beautiful messenger, Suzy, the mother of Matthew and the originator of *Matthew's Messages* and the books they have written. Go to her site www.matthewbooks.com and delve into the richness of the material that Matthew gives her, especially the book called *Matthew, Tell Me About Heaven.*

Now, what can I say today? It is kind of tricky, because some of the things I would like to say, perhaps I have said to other people and have been written in other books. They may have been said in My own God book I have just mentioned. But this Channel has not read that book in its entirety yet. Therefore, she does not know whether I have said it or not.

She just has read the second chapter where I talked about Our dear Yeshua, or Jesus to you in the Crucifixion.

She just saw how it validated her own book, *Realities of the Crucifixion*. She does not know what is beyond Chapter 2 in the God Book, so please do not think in terms of her plagiarizing anything for her integrity would not allow her to do so.

My beautiful children, one of the most difficult lessons has to do with money, I believe, for it can bring up so much of the dark energy that you may be holding or may be lurking around you. I believe it was Lady Nada in Our last book who spoke about the energy that money holds. How often have you seen people spend without any common sense, or tighten their purse strings for greed and fear—fear of lack? Do you not know, My dearest children, so precious to My heart, do you not know there is no lack? Do you not know that one of My laws is the Law of Attraction and you bring to you what you fear? Or you can bring to you what you need, what you know is there. And you can bring to you abundance. Know this deeply in your heart—know this.

This Channel has different projects buried in her heart that will take a great deal of money of which she will fund for the good of humanity. These projects are coded, and they will be opened one by one when the timing is correct.

All of you carry codes. Are you aware of this? You may say *God, what do you mean I carry a code?* I mean you have geometrical codes of Light that when they are… Hmmm, I will say that when the timing is correct, those codes explode like a seed that bursts open to bear fruit. In the jungles there are seeds that burst open when the timing is correct so that they can propagate in another place. The wind blows them.

The codings in your body are similar to that. When the timing is correct, these Light codes that carry many different purposes will explode open, and you may start to feel an urge to do something. You may start to feel that you must go some place; or you must start a new project; you must buy something. Those urges are your codes popping open—

CHRIST MICHAEL

seeds of directions, codes of Light. Each one of your bodies carries coding. It is miraculously placed in your bodies when you are in your mother's womb.

The world is a wondrous place, Readers. Take more joy in what you do. Take more moments to be joyful; take more moments to be still and allow your heart to experience peace. Take more moments to be still so you can listen, listen to the voices of your Masters and Angels and to be able to listen to Me, known by many as *God of Your Heart.*

I have given you much information in these short pages. Heed it. The information is given with purposes. And may you all hear the popping of your seed-codes that send you off scampering in all directions, scampering towards your purposes.

My love holds no bounds. I love all of you, all your colors, all the races, and yes I love the ones who have yet to find their Light.

I bless you My children. I AM you and you are Me. I AM Christ Michael.

(Thank you God, that was wonderful!) You are welcome, my dearest one.

(Author: I am amused with this chapter. I had not thought of God, or even Yeshua as being networkers! They really **are** *guiding people to various sites, where they may garner new information and/or buy spiritual books.*

I wrote a Review of the God... book for the Authors. I have put a copy of it in the Appendix.)

CHAPTER 4- DIVINE MOTHER'S THOUGHTS

Good morning to all of you once again, I AM Yeshua. It is a beautiful morning here in Arizona. For those of you who may not know, we Masters continue to watch over you. We continue to help you when you ask us; we continue to bring you our messages and teachings. It is especially gratifying to us when there is someone like this Channel who will sit and record our messages and put them into book form. That is what this Book SEVEN will be about—many teachings and wisdoms of the various Masters.

Now there is one who will be presenting today for the seventh book and our fourth chapter. I will not come back afterwards, for she plans to have quite a bit to say. (Thank you, Yeshua.)

Good morning to all of you, **I AM the Divine Mother**. I have come to give you some of my teachings and wisdom from the Goddess energies. As we have told you in previous books, and I am sure you have read here and there, eons ago the energies of humanity turned more into the masculine principle, being a patriarch society.

However, when the Earth Mother, Gaia, is evolving, she does it by bringing into balance all of her energies— the masculine as well as the feminine energies. She holds those two principles just like each of you do and your bodies do. Lady Nada has spoken about homosexuality and how that is the coming together and the recognizing of different principles and integrating them—getting you ready, you see, as you advance up that evolutionary ladder, to become androgynous. The higher Beings are not one sex or the other. You could call them an *It*, for they are in such balance. However, we do also have our preferences. I show myself

55

DIVINE MOTHER'S THOUGHTS

as a woman. I show myself as a Lady Goddess. The Mother Aspect of God is that Goddess Energy.

Yeshua, while he is balanced, he shows himself as a man. He is a male while incorporating the goddess energy. That is why he is not only wise, but he is so compassionate, so endearing to people, so loving to people because he is coming from the Goddess energy that he incorporates.

Therefore, when the world that you are living in raises her vibration, she must bring into balance the masculine and feminine principles also. You have heard so many times that we are all one. That means the world and you and we are one. The Masters and Angels and God and Goddesses, we are all one. However, we are one in a balanced way—those of higher frequencies are balanced.

What I wish to talk about today has to do with balance. When there is a part of your world that is making war on each other, coveting each other's resources, amassing large supplies of military weapons—always thinking they are under attack or getting ready to attack—they are coming from those masculine energies. That is all third dimensional. That is the patriarch reality.

As you look at some of those Middle Eastern countries, especially Iraq, the women are not allowed to be heard, let alone to be seen, as they cover themselves from head to toe. That is such an ancient way of viewing females *(third dimensional)*.

In America the people are focused on the elections. There are the two parties so far, the Democrat and the Republican. The Republican Party is very much in accord with the present president's policies. While John McCain attempts to distance himself at times, one cannot be a Republican and be far from the barn door.

In the arena of the Democratic Party we have the two senators, Hillary Clinton and Barack Obama. Each one is

56

DIVINE MOTHER'S THOUGHTS

a formidable adversary for the other. One party attempts to stay above the dark energies and the forays of the other but soon has to make explicit rebuttals to some of the things that are said.

Barack Obama is being pulled into the darker campaigning of Senator Clinton. Who will win? We cannot tell you, for it must be your own discernment and free will to choose your own president. However, we of the higher perspective can see what will happen most likely. We do not rule out the fact that another could throw his hat into the ring. It will be a hat of gold with many stars upon it, for he has earned it. It all remains to be seen.

As we look at the balance of the energies, Senator Clinton comes much from her masculine energies. When she shows her vulnerable side and sheds a few tears, she is in touch with the Goddess energies, but mostly she is not in balance for she is using the masculine part of herself to fight her battle.

Her adversary, Senator Obama, is actually more balanced on an energy level. That is why you can perceive when he is making a rebuttal that he really does not like the darker energies that are being thrown at him. His Goddess energy is more in balance with his masculine. We find it sad that people think of him as an Elitist, perhaps over- educated because he went to an Ivy League school. Consequently, people reason, he is out of touch with the common man. That type of mentality is third dimensional thinking, Readers.

Obama has a great deal of common sense, but he is being led into the quagmire by Hillary and now has to defend himself from the misguided remarks of his former pastor. Politics is not an easy game. It is not an easy game to keep your energies in balance—the masculine and feminine principles.

Back in antiquity, way back when the Goddesses were

DIVINE MOTHER'S THOUGHTS

more prevalent, when the energies were more feminine, you had the women warriors. They had strong female bodies, and they used their masculine energies to the best of their abilities. Energies have always been out of balance on this planet. It was mostly the Masters who walked this planet that would bring in the balance.

Your news media plays into the imbalance of energy by reporting so much of what they think that people want to hear, what will bring them readers, and it is mostly about crime; it is mostly centered on the wars. It is mostly centered on the movie or rock stars who are grown-up children still trying to balance their fame and fortune in their emotional body. Many have turned to addictions to help them cope.

The public buys these publications; they love the *National Inquirer*. They love to read about someone's notoriety and the details of the grisly murders. This is third dimensional, all third dimensional thinking. However, I am sure you are aware that this is all part of the transmuting process. The dark energies must rise to the top so that they can be transmuted.

When people switch channels on their TV and will not look at the violence and when people refuse to buy the publications and newspapers, refuse to listen to the local news because it is all murders and rapes, then the media may try another avenue of approach and find stories that are up-lifting and are of joy and peace.

This Channel had lunch with the delightful soul, Terri Mansfield, who is such an advocate for Peace. We watched them as they ate their lunches, healthy lunches of lettuce wraps, and brown rice with some shrimp. Terri was saying that she is a vegetarian and has been instructed to not even eat fish due to the high content of mercury. We agree. It is difficult to find any food that is pure these days.

The Jewish people have long abstained from eating shellfish of any kind for they are bottom feeders. Pollution is

DIVINE MOTHER'S THOUGHTS

getting worse; your waters are getting worse. The oceans are more and more polluted. Your food chain is becoming more polluted. When the Galactic ships come and make contact with you—as discussed in the previous book, *Your Space Brothers and Sisters Greet You*—when they are permitted to land, they will do a great deal to help you with the pollution of the waters, land, and air. It will be a few years in coming, but it will happen. In the meantime be wary of the seafood that you eat and whether it is farmed in a clean way—organically—or whether it is from polluted waters.

Watch your bodies. They are having a difficult time, for the energies that are coming onto the planet are shifting the emotional bodies. Many people read their horoscopes and are aware that the planets can influence their energy fields. But now, more so than at any time in history, the Father and the Creator are sending the new Rays and colors. These are creating tremendous shifts in the emotional, mental, and physical bodies. These bodies, especially the emotional, are having a great tug-of-war, for not only do you need to maintain your balance between the masculine and feminine energies, but you need to clear those alter-ego emotions, most of which is anger.

Anger can lead then to revenge; revenge can lead to unforgiveness. It will then loop back again to anger. So much needs to be released; much needs to be acknowledged. It is third dimensional thinking. It is the past. Bring it forward and let it go. Forgive yourself; forgive your parents; forgive your ancestors! Forgive history; forgive your leaders; forgive yourself. There is that passage, *Father forgive them for they know not what they do.* You could say *body, I forgive you;* you could say *soul I forgive you; we knew not what we did.* You did not have the information. You did not have the wisdom. You were third dimensional. You did not have the consciousness. You made soul agreements before you were born. You brought too much of your baggage with you at one time. You had the veil of forgetfulness. You were unable to

DIVINE MOTHER'S THOUGHTS

release that veil. There was so much that prevailed. Forgive yourself.

When you go back to Nirvana you will acknowledge where you have grown or perhaps failed. People need to fail at times in order to know how to win. Our dear ones, we can now make that statement that time is of the most essence in that there is not much time left for you to make your decision to get off the fence. You need to make that decision to come fully into the Light. You need to make that decision to rise above the third dimension—to be flexible, to release your belief systems. This you can do my children; this you can do.

Let us name this chapter, *The Thoughts of Your Divine Mother*. (*How about "teaching" or "wisdom?"*) NO, we like "thoughts." People can take my thoughts and turn them into wisdom if they wish—Mary's thoughts, one to another.

I will leave you now and bless you, dear Readers. We acknowledge your struggle, for life for most people is not a *bed of roses* at this time, but, oh, the rewards you will reap when you come back to us, for having been courageous enough to take on this assignment to help Earth raise her vibration, for it entails your having to raise *your* vibrations also.

My blessings to all of you, I AM the Divine Mother.

CHAPTER 5- LORD KUTHUMI- HOMOSEXUAL WORLDS

*(Chako: I just want to thank you again, Lord, for the beautiful transmissions that everybody gave last week when I/we formally presented Book SIX. They were awesome.) Yeshua: We enjoyed it also, dear one; it was awesome for us also. Now I believe this is Chapter Five that we are bringing into fruition this morning. (Yes.) So do you have a preference for someone from whom you would like to hear? (I had not thought of it in those terms. I thought **you** were bringing the Presenters forth.) But dear one, this is your book, too. How would you like to hear from Kuthumi?) Oh, my gosh, I have never channeled him for a book. That would be the greatest honor.) Then let us do so, for he is waiting here. (Oh, Michelle Eloff has just sent me his latest channeled teaching.) Then you can thank him. (Thank you.)*

I AM the Lord Kuthumi, and it is my greatest pleasure to be invited to speak as a Presenter for this book, for my understanding is that this book will be one of *Teachings*. We Masters love to teach. As many of you may know, I predominately come through my beautiful vehicle, Michelle Eloff *(Johannesburg, South Africa)*. She is a direct voice so that I am actually able to enter into her body and speak with her tongue.

However, as the Earth advances more into those higher vibrations, the ability for channels to be a direct voice will lessen. As the Earth raises her consciousness, so do all of us Masters. The higher up we go, the less that we can enter those physical bodies. Michelle has told some of you in her writings that I have received special dispensation, we shall say, from God, the Creator that allows me to continue teaching through Michelle. She is on a level that few can match. However, I can come to bodies telepathically that can

LORD KUTHUMI- HOMOSEXUAL WORLDS

reach the higher dimensions like this Channel can. She does not feel it but she is able to raise herself high enough so that as I step my energy down, we can meet.

I have taught much recently about the Unity of Consciousness and how we are one and we are not separate. We are one in Unity. If we are one, then we must also be open to the higher dimensions and to be open to our bodies' being able to balance out and incorporate the various goddesses and gods that we hold and you hold within us. I shall not repeat Michelle Eloff's teachings. It is suffice to know that each month holds particular vibrations that we Masters then can come forth and shower upon humanity. I merely am reiterating that we are emphasizing Unity Consciousness. We are emphasizing to reach deep within yourselves to bring forth that which has lain dormant within you—your feminine Goddess energies, your masculine God-like energies. Those must be incorporated; those must be blended.

It was the Divine Mother who spoke on homosexuality. I, too, will say just a short piece on that subject. People, as you go up the evolutionary ladder, your vibrations increase. You are able to go into different dimensions—the dimensions where the energy is more refined and the energy is love. The energy is non-judgment. The energy is one of integration and balance. The energy is one of joy, for a soul is joyful in its evolution. Many times people forget that growth and evolution ought to be joyful—a joyful endeavor. Therefore, if you enjoy your growth, as we Masters do, then you will be accepting of the fact that there will be times when you will need to change your outlook. You will need to readjust your belief systems.

How many of you are caught in those old teachings that homosexuality is wrong? That homosexuality is sinful? It is not a sin to love another gender. All Masters have taken physical lives in order to experience androgyny. We have taken those lives. People think of lifetimes as being only on Earth. That is not true. We have had lifetimes on different

LORD KUTHUMI- HOMOSEXUAL WORLDS

planets, as you have had. We have had lifetimes in different Universes, as some of you have had.

We have gone to planets that are strictly female. We have gone to planets that are mostly male. In that way, you see, you can say, *my gosh, that is a homosexual planet!* And I will say, *YES it is!* Those planets are set up for learning, for there is so much to learn when you are on a planet, and there is only your own gender to which you can relate. Now grant you, most of us who go to those planets for that learning situation take on that veil of forgetfulness as we are born as a woman on the female planet. You may ask how that can be? How is she fertilized? There presents the teachings, for she is able to fertilize herself. Now doesn't that sound weird? And yet it is true.

In your animal species and fish species you have those that fertilize themselves—propagate themselves. Do worms need mates? Do they mate? Of course not... Do butterflies need a mate? I'll let you think about that. However, on this planet, the higher you go up the evolutionary chain, a mate is required in order to propagate that particular species.

Yet, on the planets of which I am speaking, they evolve through their own process. On planets that are all male, they evolve. They think, *wouldn't it be nice to have a young one*? They do not think in terms of children, but in terms of a younger person, for they enjoy the youth.

I know this can be shocking to you, but there are different planets that evolve much differently than you on Earth—much differently. Therefore, when you are in that community on that planet, you do not think in terms of being a homosexual. You are what you are. You live by whatever standards have been established. There are always hierarchies in societies, for there always needs to be a leader. Sometimes this is done willingly, and sometimes through wars.

On the male-planet, they are more aggressive, for the male

energy is very strong and competitive. Therefore, there can be much fighting among themselves. As they set up different sectors on their own planet, they fight among themselves— skirmishes. Sometimes they do make dangerous weaponry, and they go charging off to another sector to dominate those people. Yet, inhabitants of a planet such as that still value life. They value life! They have their own set of laws and morals, for they also love each other.

Their physical form can be similar to those on Earth. However, they may have larger heads, or longer arms, short stature, tall stature. They will have their sexual appendages externally. In that regard they do resemble Earth's man. On some planets the males do not show a sexual appendage. So again, the physiological and biological aspects are somewhat different, for they use thought to create.

Is that not the higher way to go—to be able to create with your mind and have it happen? Is that not a more advanced society to be able to do that? What we have noticed as we study the different planets is that we need to approach each one in an absolutely non-judgmental way. And to be open to their society, to be open to their physiology, be open to their biology, and the way that they procreate. The Creator is a magnificent Being and has created many different types of Intelligences—Universes upon Universes too numerous to count.

I, Kuthumi, have yet to be able to explore all that is out there. Do you think that I have gone to all 700 Universes and all planets in every one of those 700 Universes? We will just say *not yet*, for each one is an adventure and each one has its own dimensions so that you could visit one for a million years and not see it all because you did not get through all of the dimensions. The people on Earth are apt to forget because they are in their finite minds and are apt to forget all the different ways that Creator has created.

I have talked about the male-planet. There are not just

LORD KUTHUMI- HOMOSEXUAL WORLDS

one; there are many, many more. They are apt to be numbered versus having a name, for your Astronomers would be scrambling to find it saying, *give us a name; give us a name; give us the quadrants.* I will not do that.

Now let us look at a planet that is only female. These planets propagate themselves also by thought. But they carry the babies within and give birth to them, while on the male-planet the gestation period is one of thought and then the new form appears. They send it Light and work with it helping it to become stronger.

The females have the babies by giving birth in a similar fashion as here on Earth. However, the birth is very easy. They have the gestation period and when it is time, the body opens up and the baby is released. There is no pain. Many times they give birth in water and then bring the beautiful baby girl out of the water. There are all shapes and sizes in that society also. You would be surprised how a woman whom you would consider obese would be looked upon as one of beauty on some of these planets.

Each planet has its own government, its own set of rules, its own Moses (*Kuthumi chuckles, for he was Moses*), its own prophets. Therefore, in that way, they are similar to Earth people also.

Now what was my objective in telling you all of this this morning? It was to give you Readers a new perspective on homosexuality, for this will help to break down the old stereotypes, break down what the church Fathers have labeled as *sin*. It is doubtful if there will come a time in your generation where same-sex marriages will be acceptable. However, on these planets I was telling you about, there is no other way of being.

You find each other and have a relationship. Now those marriages would not be like they are on Earth. You could put them more into the category of mating for life. Some mate for life. Some hop around (*chuckles*)—a bee buzzing, gathering nectar.

We Masters feel many times that people are willing to change their belief systems if enough information is given to them so that they can see different points of view. However, those Fundamental churchgoers will not change certain points of view because their pastors or priests will not change *their* points of view. Thereby, all are stuck in their way of seeing society. They are stuck.

People who have died and passed on and are in Nirvana come over at the stage they were in when they left their body. They may not even rise enough to have that belief system change. Only your higher soul is all- knowing—your Oversoul is all-knowing. Your other souls may not be. It is the task of the Oversoul to bring all the souls that it put out back to the Oversoul with consciousness. You can think of it like a great migration—everybody migrating to go Home. Then, when you are Home, there is great excitement, and there can be a pilgrimage to other planets—to other worlds, to other ways of being, to other ways of stepping up that ladder to other Universes.

Homosexuality, Readers, is such a miniscule way of perceiving your world. Think in terms of androgyny. Other Universes allow them to have their own society and do not judge them. There will always be a comparison, but to compare, let it be one of interest and delight in how the Creator has created something that you have not even thought of—how absolutely delightful!

Now since I cannot ask for questions because there is no one else here but this Channel, I will close and will be watching when you read these words in this Book SEVEN. It has been truly my delight to speak with you.

I AM Kuthumi.

(*Oh Lord, thank you very much for coming. That was*

LORD KUTHUMI- HOMOSEXUAL WORLDS

quite informative for me also.) Yes, I thought it would be informative for many people. It is my greatest pleasure to work with you. I work with you each month as you work and digest the information that my vehicle, Michelle Eloff, sends you. I am most gratified. Blessings, dear one, blessings. (*Thank you Lord Kuthumi*.) 5-20-08

CHAPTER 6 - YESHUA- AA MICHAEL

Precious Readers, good morning to you, we are back once again to present another chapter and to give you a new teaching. We have just had Kuthumi who provided a new perspective on androgyny and homosexuality for you.

You see, when we Masters speak on these controversial subjects, it broadens your outlook. It touches your belief systems, and if you can accept what we are telling you as truth, then your belief systems start to change. For this particular book, it is our objective to help you change those belief systems that are programmed into you by your well-meaning grandparents, perhaps, parents, siblings, peers, grade school teachers, professors, pastors, and rabbis— all the various people who provided you with different information. Authors and their books have also given you information throughout your formative years.

Many of you now are in your senior years—as you are what we would call the baby-boomers, having been born in the 1940s. You have accrued much wisdom. However, how much of that knowledge is truth or how much of that knowledge is from others that is only half-truths—those beliefs that you have taken on?

If you are ready to let go of some of the religiosity that has been taught you, if you are ready to let go of some of the political discussions that you have been flooded with over these past months, if you are ready to change political parties, then you are ripe to read these books. You have been well honed, and you now are open to new ideas.

This Channel sends out the information that we have given her far and wide and amazingly enough the relatives of her extended family are having the most difficulties accepting some of the new ideas she puts forth and has written in the books.

To us, different sectors of the United States, different states are more programmed into stereotypical ways of thinking than other states are. California has always been a progressive state. It has the reputation of having the flower children, marijuana and the Peace marchers—the openness to new ideas—during the 1960s-1970s.

Then there is the Bible belt down through Texas and the neighboring states. They are so sure their religion is the absolute truth. On the political scene, you have the Republicans and the Democrats. Each one is expounding his or her truth. How does one discern? It becomes most difficult, does it not?

Sometimes the younger generation is not so cemented into certain concepts. They do draw their own ideas, but they are more open. They have a broader range of ideas coming in because they are so proficient on the Internet. They have so much bombarded into their psyches from the different tunes and songs that they listen to, the different dance steps that they watch and learn on TV.

The older generation struggles because they do not understand the Rap music, the Hip-Hop dancing. Most of them do not even like it. They do not understand the messages that are conveyed. Therefore, each generation is a learning experience for all. And what we are talking about, people, is growth in consciousness, are we not? How can you grow in consciousness if you are not willing to change your belief systems?

There is so much information here that may seem controversial to each one of you who reads these books, for it does not agree with what you have been told or you have been led to believe. It is Festinger's Cognitive Dissonance all over again—you feel unrest in your psyche until you make the decision as to what side of the fence you wish to be on. Then the cognitive dissonance dies down and you feel at peace once again.

*Cognitive dissonance is an excellent way to perceive a belief system that perhaps is not flexible, for when you hear truth and you carry the same truth, there is no dissonance. However, when you hear someone else's truth and it does not agree with your own, then your mind rejects it and/or your body reacts to it. You tell yourself, there is something **off**. Who do I believe?*

*We often have said you need to believe your own truth. However, the question arises how do we know when our truth is really not the truth? Ah, that is where discernment comes into play. It is only by growing in consciousness that you can begin to distinguish the real truth from all others that are bombarding the planet. Some truths are easier to discern than others, for they immediately resonate with you. We can only tell you to be flexible. Do not immediately shut down your mind to a new idea, for you may be hearing a truth for the first time that is **the** truth. Be flexible, dear souls; be willing to change.*

The Presenter of this new chapter will be one you have heard from before. He has asked if he may speak again, for he is very ancient. We could say he is an old, old Being and very wise. He is millions of years old and you will know him. So I will step aside now and let him come forth.

Good morning. Once again we meet, dear Readers. **I AM** the **Archangel Michael**. Yes, I have been around your galactic space for many eons. You know, each Being of the higher evolution has a *spiritual gang*, as we call it. I am part of this Channel's *gang*, along with Yeshua, Lady Nada, Mary Magdalene, Holy Mary, and yes, even God is a part of her gang. There are others who have not introduced themselves to her yet. Each spiritual gang member comes forth when there has been conscious recognition that he or she is with

71

the person. Saint Germain is also part of her gang, as you have been told before. And the list is growing. She has a prominent Hindu who as yet to make himself known.

Therefore, you see, each of you Readers has your own spiritual gang members. Is it not wonderful to be able to use that term and to know that it is of the highest, spiritual, conscious, Christ energy, love, peace, and joy that there is? Not one of us carries a gun. As you know, dear friends, my sword is symbolic because in your way of perceiving life, a knife or a sword cuts things. I am able to cut through cords and energies and things of that nature. This gives you something to think about regarding who your gang members are. Of course, we do get around. This is not the only Channel to whom I come. A gang is not exclusive. I belong to many gangs, and it is quite humorous when you think of it in those terms.

Is it not sad when one cannot think of a gang member in those higher vibrations? For the majority of you, a gang member is one that is depicted on TV or in the news media or in different neighborhoods that you may know of. They are looked down upon; they are frowned at, for so many times their energy is so dark. They pierce their body with rings and tattoos. Some carry dangerous weaponry—knives that can slash off a finger or stab you to death, guns that can blow a hole through you the size of a melon. Those are the dark energies. Those gangs are not of the Light. While they are still part of God's children, He does have some *black sheep* (if you want to use that term) in His family.

Our gangs on our level are of the Light. Actually, *gang* is such a human term that we do not use it in the higher realms. However, I wanted to give you a different picture so you could conceptualize another way of looking at gangs.

Your political scene is heating up. There are three people still running. One is truly a shining Light (*Senator Barack Obama*). One is a tenacious mavrick. While his courage is admirable, he is not able to rise above the failing (*Republican*) party (*Senator John McCain*). The woman candidate is fighting a hard battle (*Senator Hillary Clinton*). It is a valiant effort, an effort and a struggle to stay in control. The more that she and her husband see the opportunity slipping away from them, the harder she fights and the more vicious become her attacks on her opponents. (*Senator Obama*) is learning how to play as he goes along—how to face the challenges when you are running for office. If you are running for president, that makes you fair game for the people to pounce upon and for the media to scrutinize. Every action, every word—**every** word that someone has said to you—is fair game.

How many of you could stand the scrutiny that these candidates must go through? I would be willing to say that there is an area in each of your lives that you would not like to be known publicly. Does that make you a bad person? Does that make you a wrong person? NO, not unless that area was one involving a terrible crime. It makes you human. The candidate I am talking about is the younger man, of course (*Senator Obama*). He is full of Light, and it is the dark tentacles from the opposing candidates and the opposing party that are attacking him. There is that saying; *all is fair in love and war*. It looks as if that could apply to politics also, for some political games are war-like.

Suzanne Ward in her latest message from Matthew (*May 21, 2008*) stated that this young man, Senator Barack Obama, would win the presidency. However, it is the people's free will (*as to who will win*). Each person must look deeply into his/her heart and see why he or she would not vote for this Senator. He is a just man. He has a beautiful soul. He is intelligent, far above the average intelligence of most people and yes, he is in a human body and has much to learn about foreign politics. However, he is a quick learner. He is an orator. And he has a great deal of common sense.

You must know by now that your wisdom needs to be

tempered by common sense. What good is it to have your ideals up in the sky if you do not have any common sense to go with them? Barack has a beautiful family. His wife also is a very high Being—one of Light. His two small children are Light Beings themselves. This is a family of Light, America. We have put legions of angels around this family.

You are familiar with this Channel's other books in which Ashtar has said that she is on their radar screen and they are looking out for her. Senator Obama and his family also are on the radar screen on one of the ships. It may surprise you to know that there is a ship in another dimension following him. He may not see it, but the ship is following him and keeping him and his family safe. (*I believe they are watching over Senator McCain also.*)

This Channel gave an hour's discussion a week or so ago, and she spoke about believing the cloud that the Hebrews saw as they traversed the desert for forty years was really a *cloud ship*—a spaceship surrounded by what would look like a cloud. It followed them and rained down manna to them. And yes, it was God in that ship directing them.

Now the Galactic Command's space technology has advanced, just like humanity's has. You no longer have the Model T Ford to drive around in. You have great technology in cars these days. The same applies to the Command. Their ships have much more capability than they had in those Biblical times. Therefore, those people of the Light are on the radar screen. As Matthew—that soul of Light—said to his mother Suzy Ward, Obama and his family are greatly protected... and so they are.

This chapter is somewhat diverse today. Yeshua talked about belief systems and now I have spoken. Take heed, People; let truth come in. Change your belief systems. Talk to your gang.

I AM Archangel Michael.

YESHUA- AA MICHAEL

All right dear one, you have a question about the *Course in Miracles*. (*Yes, one of my "fans" wanted to know if you had written that Course? It made me stop and think because Barbara Marciniak's Master said it was a "mind-control game" from the government. So now I am thinking, "Oh gosh, who is right here?"*) Dear one, your government did put out a version of the *Course in Miracles*, but what has not been told was that we were able to intercede and re-write some of it. Therefore, when the government people were writing what they thought was mind-control, we Masters were in there putting in our energy and writing it also.

Consequently, you had our version superimposed on their version. That is why people are led to it. When Heather (*my editor*) told you that Mana (*a spiritually advanced Being*) had said that the *Course* was not mind-control, that is because we had over-laid it! (*I've never heard of such a thing, chuckling.*) *Yeshua cracks up laughing.* Dear one, there is much that you have not heard of! And that is just one of them. We over-laid that *Course.* Now why Barbara Marciniak's Master said otherwise, we do not know.

However, hear this, dear one, I, Yeshua would be absolutely in agreement if a student wished to study the *Course in Miracles*. It is beautiful. It is a beautiful book. You can tell your "fan" that it was written not only by me, but with other Masters. Remember we never come alone; it is always a joint effort. The *Course in Miracles* was written by the Ascended Masters—over-laid on what the mind-control people were writing. You can tell her both versions so that she can make up her own mind, but the *Course* is beautiful— the energy is beautiful. It has helped many people.

Is that enough information for you? (*Yes, I would never have thought of that in a million years, chuckling.*)

All right, dear one, you have your work cut out for you

to type this entire Chapter 6 up. We will meet with you at another time.

Greetings.

CHAPTER 7- BLUE STAR SPEAKS

Dearest one, I AM Yeshua back again. As you flip from page to page, I hope all of you Readers will think of us coming into this Channel's energy field and delivering a teaching or message for all of you. It is heartwarming for us, and we appreciate it so much. We thank you for reading the book and passing on the information.

We enjoy the e-mails that this Channel receives. She recently received one from the UK from an elderly gentleman. He felt starved for the truth that we had spoken about in Book FOUR, about the Realities of the Crucifixion. He was so thankful, for he had searched long and wide for true information (about Jesus).

Therefore, when we see that our information is fanning out wider and wider, it is very gratifying for us. We send that gentleman our love. When he reads this book, he will know whom we are talking about. His wife is slower to respond. She prefers the Bible over the truth in our books. She will come around one of these days.

You see, Readers, no one can make the other person step up onto another rung of the ladder in his or her evolution— that rung to a higher consciousness. No one can make you do that. What we are speaking about is soul's work. That is soul's growth and each soul grows at a different pace, through different information, and through a different process. While it can be difficult for partners when it looks as if one has out-stepped the other, patience must enter in and of course always be accompanied by love. We are not all quick to learn—a quick study. Some of the souls are quicker than others, but in other aspects some may have stepped forth before their partner has—each at his or her own pace, Beloveds. Always

BLUE STAR SPEAKS

remember that. You cannot change your partners; you cannot change your neighbors. You can change only yourself.

*Now today, we have a surprise for all of you, for we are going to step aside and let a great Being from another star system speak with you. He calls himself Blue Star, The Pleiadian. He comes through different people, but mainly through his daughter, Celestial Blue Star, who has a physical body on Earth. It is she who suggested to this Channel, "Why don't you channel my father, Blue Star?" It had never occurred to this Channel that she ought to or could channel this great Being. Therefore, we will let you be the judge, as I announce with the greatest affection, "Here is **Blue Star from the Pleiades**."*

(Chako: Blue Star, with all respect, I need to check you out, please. "I now demand in the name of Jesus The Christ to know if you are a Being of the Jesus The Christ Consciousness, if you are a Being of the true God of the God Light Consciousness of the Creator, answer me, YES, or NO.")

YES, our dear Chako and it is good to speak with you! We have conversed many times in what you call the *ethers.* However, I thought it was time to speak to you on what we will call a *professional basis.* Therefore, I come to you, and I come through these pages of this book so that the Readers may read what I have to say to them.

My daughter, Celestial, and her husband, David of Arcturus, have websites on the Internet. They post my teachings. There is much to choose from if you go to that site (www.bluestarspeaks.com). Please do so, for it is my belief that truth needs to be spoken. Truth needs to reign on this Earth.   Too many times there have been what I call the *False Prophets* expounding on their own ideas and their own interpretations of truth. On our site, Celestial, David and I have spoken on this subject matter. It bears repeating in this book.

BLUE STAR SPEAKS

As you have noticed, this Channel (*first*) read this little blurb to me to check me out, to hear me say that YES, I am a Being of Light from the Creator. People, you need to make this your daily practice when you are channeling Beings. Even if God came to you and said, "I AM God," you are to check Him out; read the little blurb that Sananda himself had written and given to Celestial. It is on our website (*under "Introduction to the Saga of the False Prophets." At the end of that article you can click to view "Checking Sources and Aligning Energy." Sananda's information is there.*)

There is an observation I would like to present to you this morning. It is one where people are slow in making a decision as to what side of the fence they are going to jump onto. People are just sitting on the fence. They keep weighing the different energies, wondering which way they ought to jump. Those dark energies have manipulative tentacles, and they know your Achilles Heel. They know how to approach you, how to ensnare you. They are clever. They are masterful. They are of the dark. They are Illuminati. If you wish to be on that side of the fence, then it is time to make your decision. Stop vacillating. I, of course, would prefer that all would come to the Light. However, there are still those who are emotionally immature. They like playing with fire. They like playing with the Ouija board. They like testing the waters, the dark waters.

People, your world is raising her vibration, and those who cannot rise with her will be sent to another planet. If you think that will be all wine and roses, think again. How many of you know of people who are in gangs of the darker energy? They put their toe in and then are drawn into it deeper and deeper. The gang members say one must do this or that so that others will know that you really want to be one of them.

The sons and daughters of God who are not emotionally secure are apt to go ahead and cave in from peer pressure. Do you not know that one must stand strong and firm in truth—stand steadfast in the Light of God? How many of you reading this book clearly understand that principle? How many of you totally agree? If you have waffled for even a second, let that be a hint to you that you still have not made a total commitment to go to the Light and stand steadfast in the Light and be fully into the Christ Consciousness.

This decision comes to every person in this world. This decision is Universal. Come to the Light, for if you make that choice to go toward darkness, it will consume you inch by inch. You will be consumed. You will lose your identity. You will be merged into those dark emotions and into that dark way of being.

All children of God are born into the Christ Consciousness. All children carry that. When they come into their body and are actually in the Earth's energies, they start losing touch with that Light. It depends so much upon whom their parents are—who is bringing them into the world.

There has been an increase of walk-ins as the Earth raises her vibrations. That is because the souls do not have the time to come in as babies. Souls think of that as wasting 20 years or more before they can start their work. Even old souls are stepping into older bodies. This has been a practice for eons of time. The purpose of the walk-ins is to bring in a higher consciousness into the body on a soul agreement with the soul who is leaving the body. That soul was a caretaker for that body.

As he or she left after having prepared the body for 20 plus years, the next soul could come in with stronger energy, a deeper potency and be able to start spiritual work immediately. You see the bodies that the walk-ins are coming into now are fairly strong bodies. They are younger bodies. Many times the body has not died from a disease but maybe has died from a drowning so that the body remains intact when it has been revitalized by the newer soul—(*the new occupant, not a new versus an old soul*). The bodies are

BLUE STAR SPEAKS

strong; they are vibrant and can hold a great deal of energy. These walk-ins are of the highest level of consciousness. Many of them are Masters. Many of them can recall the fact that they have walked into a body. Many of them take on the karmic debt of that body, but they are able to accomplish that quickly and with less drama than the previous owner would have had to go through.

The walk-ins have a higher intelligence, but when they are in the body, there is much programming to be released. There is much re-wiring of the brain to be done in order to allow the soul to bring in the higher level of learning and discernment and just being.

How many of you sitting on the fence are contemplating suicide? It has been noted that there has been a higher rate of suicides among the young Army soldiers returning from the wars. Many of those suicides are done through drugs or through guns, which harms the body immensely so that a walk-in is not able to use that body. Would that not have been a wonderful exchange to give your body to a higher Being? When you vacated, you had left a strong body. The new Being that comes in can adjust the emotions, for you see **it** was not part of the emotional trauma. Therefore, it can override that fairly easily.

Readers, never commit suicide. Stay in the Light. This government has not done well by the veterans that are returning. The medical help is inadequate. Many of these young men and women need counseling but are not receiving that much. They wish to further their education and yet the government is giving them barely enough (*money*) to make it through a year's schooling and certainly not enough for your Ivy-League schools. There is not much justice these days that we see in the world.

People, there is not that much time to vacillate. You must make your decisions. Most people who read these books have made that decision to stay in the Light. However, you see, they have extended family members who may not be going towards the Light as much as they need to. People are not working on developing the spiritual side of life because they equate it with religion.

As you know, the religions of this world do not hold that much truth. The religions of this world can actually hold you back. Odd as it may sound, it is in the more spiritually minded studies where one learns different ways (*modalities*) of thinking. This Channel is a graduate of Transpersonal Psychology. It is a psychology that allows one to go beyond ego and to accept alternative realities. I find it amusing that one would receive more information that would help you in your spiritual life by studying a course in Transpersonal Psychology than one would studying the Bible sitting in a church!

One could say, *what has gone wrong here*? But then that person would need to recognize that the religions went off balance eons ago. Even when Moses brought down the laws, the Hebrews were not ready to hear them. Every religion that has sprung from one of the more prominent teachers that walked your planet has failed—the religions have failed you because the dark energies got into them. Brothers were killing brothers, raping sisters, looting from the churches, from the synagogues, from the temples with greed. All was in the name of "**my** god is the true God. Your god is the false one. My prophet is the one of truth. Your prophet is the one of darkness. Therefore, let's crucify him."

When you look back on thousands of years of history, there is not one religion left today from the original Cell of God—the Seed of God, the true religion. It was bent (*distorted from truth*) from the very beginning. The Zealots and even the Prophets turned from the truth, making their ego the new teachings. **No religion is truth!**

Now are there kernels of wisdom here and there? Of course, but they are so mixed in with the chaff that they are hardly recognizable. Even that great Lord of Lords, Yeshua/ Sananda, teaching people to *love thy neighbor*... the message has become distorted. *Well if our neighbor is a drug addict, how can we love him?* And yet, he/she is a child of God. Sananda knew at that time that all humanity was a child of God.

Sitting on the fence, People, reading erroneous Bibles, staying glued to your stereotypical ways of thinking and your belief systems and refusing to change—these are the ingredients for failure—for failing to come to the Light. However, they can and will be your passage to a new planet if that is your desire—a planet that is full of your peers, who think like you do, who look like you do in most ways, and who smell like you do with decay and no Light. That planet is waiting for you. You have a choice, you fence sitters. Make that choice soon; make it soon.

I AM Blue Star of the Pleiades, and it has been my greatest pleasure to speak to you and to have my words conveyed by this Channel of truth.

Salude.

(Thank you, Blue Star; it was very strong and potent. How would you like me to name this chapter?) I think make it very simple: *Blue Star Speaks* ought to suffice. *(Thank you.)* You are welcome, dear child of Light. You are most welcome. Salude. *(Hmmm, thank you for coming, I am honored.)*

Well dear one that was our friend from a neighboring star system. His energy was quite magnificent; was it not? *(Yes, it seemed to get stronger and stronger the more he talked.)* That is because he was able to come closer.

All right dear one, that's it for today. *(Thank you Yeshua.)* You are welcome. Greetings.

CHAPTER 8- WORDS of MARY MAGDALENE

*Good morning everyone, and as I was saying to this Channel, "Your Gang's all here!" as she was listening to some lovely spiritual music (*A Treasury of Hymns CD presented through Benny Hinn Ministries, 2005*). We are ready to start the next chapter. We have been having very powerful Beings speak, but they do carry more of the masculine principle* (though they are balanced)*, so we think it is time to switch to the feminine principle and have one of our Regulars come forth.*

The Channel was reading some material put out by Michelle Eloff, that superb Channel, the vehicle that Kuthumi, I, Mary Magdalene and many, many others use (www.thelightweaver.org). While reading what Mary Magdalene had written, guess who popped in (chuckles)? Of course, it is my beloved, Mary Magdalene. She will be the next Presenter.

Good morning, precious Readers and to this Channel. It is I, **Mary Magdalene**. Some of you may know me as **Lady Nada**. I have several aspects, as do all of you. You just do not know the names of your higher selves. Won't you be surprised when you finally learn that you are Lady so and so, or Lord so and so? Many of you are Masters, you know—Lady Masters and male Masters.

You came to this planet for this specific purpose, to work in these years of the 2000 millennium, and it is 2008 as I speak. You came specifically to help Gaia—Mother Earth—to raise her vibratory rate. You see, it is always a two-way street. You are helping her, and by her wishing to raise her vibration, you are able to raise yours. You are bringing forth your **past** experiences. You are getting in touch with your **present** experiences. You are bringing more joy into your life. You are bringing more love into your life. You are bringing more Light into your life. That is what this lifetime is for. That is what it is all about. We often have said that when you help us, we help you.

When you as a child of God—and I am speaking of the adult child of God—decide you are going to climb that ladder to higher evolution, when you decide that you have had enough of fear, thank you, no more fear, when you decide to give up some of your narcissistic ways, if not all of your narcissism, when you decide to leave ego behind and come forward into a greater Light, when you decide all of that, then you are raising your vibratory rate. You are seeking a higher dimension.

You have been told the Earth is going forward. She wishes to reside more and more in those higher dimensions. She wishes that all Beings that occupy her lands would be from higher consciousness. The originality of this planet was to have a blending of Heaven and Earth. It was and is to be for the higher Masters of Light to come and walk on this planet and experience again its beauty in a physical body— in a physical, touching manner.

And, YES, we visit many times, but we are in our spiritual bodies. To us, it is not always clearly experienced in a tactile way. Saint Germain once told this Channel that that is what he misses. YES, he is doing beautiful work and is a high Master, but he misses being able to use the human senses that one can have in a physical body walking the Earth. The Masters of the higher Realms cannot lower their energy enough to walk physically on your planet—in the flesh. This is what we want to do. It would be similar to your going to a beautiful island such as the Hawaiian Islands before the commercialism took over.

We want a beautiful land where the waters run clear and pure, where the flowers bloom in abundance, where the weather is mild and there are slight breezes. Everything is clean and pristine. The sunlight comes down and it warms you, versus burning you; the rains gently come down and wash you, versus flooding you out; the wind blows gently, versus blowing in a rage and destroying everything in its path. That is not to be again. That is our dream. That is the Creator's creation—God's creation—to have a beautiful planet where we can vacation, to use your term; we can vacation and find much joy walking among all of you.

It will be a place where my dearest Lord Yeshua/Sananda can sit once again on a little knoll and speak with you. However, he will be speaking with you as peers and not as people in their second and third dimension, groveling for him, straining to take pieces of his garment, straining to take pieces of him in that "taking" energy.

Visualize, People, what it will be like when these great Masters can come and gather you to them like a family. You are their extended family, and there will be joyous reunions. There will be such respect, each person respecting the other with love. That is what you are all a part of creating for Mother Earth. You are creating a vacation spot where even God can take a body and walk His beloved Gaia. What a joy that will be. That is creating joy, dear ones; that will be most joyous.

Your planet is such a dear soul. She is gentle. Are you aware of that? She is gentle and loving. She has been taken advantage of by what we will call the *lesser gods*, the masses who do not appreciate what they have. They do not appreciate their bodies. Their bodies many times are covered in tattoos and are pierced by rings and dotted with fake diamonds. Some are real diamonds in their nose.

Oh, People, how some of you have forgotten the sacred trust that you had agreed to when you took your body. There are veils of forgetfulness, yes, but then there are veils that people never attempt to pierce in order to awaken. They pass over to the other side and see what a folly their life was. It was a caricature; it was laughable, if it were not so painful to see when they have that review in their afterlife.

If you could see the souls that we see after they have had their review, you could see that very few are joyous and happy with how they had led their life—very few, for they always see where there could have been a different way of experiencing.

This Channel is playing that old, old hymn, *Onward Christian Soldiers,* on a CD in the background. Those times to us were so long ago. They were so painful, although we do not look at them that much. However, just like all of you may do when you hear certain pieces of music, it brings up memories. I am near this body and listening to that old time hymn, which one could say is not politically correct anymore, but it was this Channel's favorite hymn when she was a little girl. It brought forth the memories, you see, of when she was with her beloved Brother. Those memories are deeply engrained with her.

Many of you have such memories of those Biblical times. However, your task this lifetime is to rise above the religiosity of your teachings, is it not? It is a time to let go of all of those belief systems. It was Blue Star, that magnificent Being from the Pleiades, who was telling you that none of the religions hold absolute truth—none of them do. Readers, if you learn nothing else from this book, please learn that. None of those religions speak **the** truth.

The Torah does not speak total truth. The Jews are similar to Christians who hold on to every single word in their Bible. They all have such difficulty in embracing the concept that what they are reading and believing is not (*total*) truth. People, believe me when I say your present day religions are not the way to go to enhance your spirituality, for the seeker of truth knows the scriptures in the Christian Bible hold little truth.

WORDS of MARY MAGDALENE

For the layperson it is very difficult to find the kernels of truth among all the chaff. Most simply are not there. Most simply are disguised by the scribes with their own conjectures, concepts, and ego. You have been told many times through these different books that the scribes put their own spin on everything. Even people who channel today do not always make a clear delineation between what they are channeling and their own interpretation. This Channel strives to her utmost to be true to the words that are spoken. If there needs to be a change of a word, she puts that into parentheses in italics so that you will know that she is giving more clarification. Therefore, you see it is very easy for scribes to change a word here or there, especially if they do not read it correctly or if they do not hear it correctly. They then put in what they **think** has been said. This is what scribes did thousands of years ago (*and still do.*)

I wish to tell you, Readers, that this is the time in your life that you have chosen. This is the time that you told God when you took this body that you would follow through on your purpose of holding the Light. Now some Beings have a more prominent task than others. Certainly the major candidate running for president in America has a major task. He is Senator Barack Obama. Now there have been TV commentators that denigrate him because he has not agreed with them. However, I, Mary Magdalene, am telling you he is **the one**. He is the one to lead America forward.

He is over-lighted by Abraham Lincoln, who comes full circle. President Lincoln had the war to liberate the slaves and to give freedom to all. Now he has come back to over-light a black man who will lead the people to freedom, for they have lost their freedom from the previous administration (*George W. Bush*). Now is that not a perfect karmic circle? Do you not see that? It is perfect in our eyes.

Many of you will not agree with me. Many of you will ponder this and use your discernment, for my truth may not be your truth. But know, dear Readers, that no one in a body is perfect, for you are bombarded by the energies of the planet and by the energies of others around you. Does Senator Obama always say what would be beneficial to everyone? Most likely not. But do you? Someone was expressing to this Channel that he did not think Senator Obama was an orator for he was so hesitant lately in how he speaks. Wouldn't you? He is weighing every word he says. He knows what he means, but if he slips and says the wrong word, he is crucified in the press. It is not an easy position.

Some people fear for his life, for here is a black man attempting to be the president of the United States. There are still many people in your country, dear Readers, who had past lives on those southern plantations, who carry that southern mentality to their very core, and they abhor the fact that a black man could be their president. They tolerate a black man if he is mayor, if he is governor of a state, if he is a TV commentator, if he is a noted author (if *he is a Congressman or Senator*), but that is too big of a stretch for them to have a black president. However, we are delighted. It is such a perfect example of karma coming full circle.

How many of your karmic pieces have come full circle? You have all had lives as black people—all of you! There is not one of you who has not been all colors and creeds—not one of you (*said with great emotion*). If you can accept that concept, you will then know that of course you are seeing karma being played out in front of your eyes. When he is sworn in as president that will be Abraham Lincoln's greatest delight. He is Barack Obama fulfilling his purpose and his pledge to God and his higher souls. Always know, Readers, **you** have been all colors of the skin.

This Channel was a Holy Man in Africa for several lifetimes. She then came over in another lifetime as a black slave in one of the slave ships. She/he was in one of those little cages that were one on top of the other for days in that long voyage that ended in being sold in slavery. Most of you have had past lives like that. You have honed who you are by those types of lifetimes. They have honed you and have made you the superb Being that you are today.

It is always rather ironic. Some people hate the Jews. Well guess what—you were one! Some people hate the Mexicans. Well guess what—you were one. Some people hate the Chinese. Guess what—you were one. And interestingly enough, all of you played those games not only once but several times through all the spectrums of a particular game. You did it and then as you go up that evolutionary ladder, you more or less settle on what you look like and what (*and where*) you will be. However, on your evolutionary journey, if you are to be in Tibet for a particular reason, that is where you will go!

The games are not all played out yet. There is still much to be done before Heaven is truly a part of Mother Earth. Ponder this, dear souls. Bring those lives forward; bring them forward with joy and know that YES, I have done that. YES, I did that and look at me now! You are magnificent souls. You are courageous Beings. You are Beings of Light, but you are still growing as all of us are.

Let go of thinking about those Biblical players and putting them in a box as **the** Holy Family. Let go of that. Each of us is an individual and that was thousands of years ago. We are who we are today. We are not who we were then. We are energy of Light and many times we have no form, but strictly energy of Light. Think of us that way, my beloved souls. We are one, and you too are energies of Light.

It has been my greatest pleasure, and I bless all of you. I wish you the greatest joy and love and Light that you can possibly attain and can contain. (We will call this chapter the *Words of Mary Magdalene*.)

I AM Mary Magdalene. Au revoir.

(*Thank you, Mary, it was potent per usual.*) You are welcome my blessed friend; you are welcome.

CHAPTER 9 - EARTH MOTHER GAIA

Good morning everybody, it is I, Yeshua, and many other Beings that come with me. This Channel has had a few days off as she pursued some projects that were pending, so she has not sat for a few days. Thereby, it is good to be back.

*Now we have Chapter 9 coming up, and we would like to bring a Being forth who has yet to be a part of our book, although she definitely **is** a part of our book. She is Mother Earth; she is Gaia. She is very definitely a part of anything that happens on her planet. I will bring her forth.*

(Gaia, I need to check you out. "I now demand in the name of Jesus the Christ..." Gaia answered YES to the query that Sananda had composed for checking out Beings before one channels them, so I let her continue.)

Good morning Readers, I am your planet speaking. Some call me **Mother Earth**; some call me **Gaia**. I have many forms (*names*), and it is interesting and an honor for me to be invited to speak. This Channel was musing a few days ago and thinking to herself. "Now who would be another wonderful person to be a Presenter for this book?" And she thought, "Why, Gaia, that would be great!" So here I am.

As you know, there are areas of me all over the world that are in flux. They are in the process of changing. Since this Channel lives in America, we will speak about what is going on in America. Right now there is massive flooding going on in Indiana. I know that it poses a hardship for people there. However, if you can change your outlook and think of it as an adventure, know that this is all necessary. The waters will bring sediment to the fields, but it is also washing the energy of the cities (*and neighboring areas*).

As I raise my vibration and go up the ladder, just as all of

EARTH MOTHER GAIA

you are, into a higher dimension, I too need to change. Each of you changes your belief systems so that you can advance. I as a planet must change my body (as actually all of you must change your bodies also). However, my body consists of all of you living among the folds of my bosom, shall we say. You are in my arms along with my beloved animals, the vegetation, the foliage, and the flowers. All of you are a part of me.

As you have been told repeatedly, and I am sure you recognize this by now, there are sections of this body of mine that need to lighten up. How I do that is with shaking myself around a little. This causes tremors, tsunamis, releasing old pent-up energies—dark energies—from man/woman's over-zealous acts of greed, treachery, possession, all the lower bases of consciousness.

People speak so much of how one is acting like an animal while some of the animals are so true to their nature, so beautifully aligned and balanced with harmony in their hearts and the fierce protectiveness of their mates. Yet man/woman of your species kill your mates, abandon your children, abuse your children. Now I know there are animals in the Animal Kingdom that play a similar game, but I am speaking to the human race right now, to your level of consciousness. You bring not only harm to yourself, but to me! I speak of the harm that you have done me! I have asked for help from God and the Creator. "Help, I need more Light." Your space brothers and sisters help provide this. Everybody has brought me new energies so that I am starting to feel hopeful. I am starting to feel that there is a probability that all will be well.

As a planet, it is my purpose to provide sustenance to all those who inhabit me—sustenance for the Animal Kingdom and for the human race. So many times when drastic changes need to be made, drastic measures come into play beforehand. As I shake and rattle, think of a large, shaggy dog shaking the fleas, the dark energies off of its back.

EARTH MOTHER GAIA

You see, Readers, these energies are from thousands of years ago. We are speaking of thousands of years of abuse, other people's consciousness, and other people destroying me. When the trees are chopped down to provide shelter or to just to clear the land for planting, each tree is then killing a part of me—each felled tree. You have all been told ad infinitum that the oxygen for me and for you… (*is provided by the trees*).

In your oceans, the great whales that people have harpooned and killed unconsciously for their oil and meat… do they not realize they are killing Light? These great cetaceans anchor the Light into my body. I would be much darker than I am now if it were not for the whales and the dolphins anchoring the Light in my oceans.

Pesticides, Readers, also poison me. People in this desert area of Arizona spray their houses and foundations against termites, (*ants*), and other insects entering into their houses. The products are toxic and they do poison me. However, I realize that humans do not have a consciousness yet to know how to work with the insect kingdom, to set boundaries so that the insects will not come and feast on the foundations of their houses. I cannot excuse any of this, but I can accept some of it, for the more conscious people lay a fine line around the foundation of their houses or patios and do not extend the pesticide into the whole yard. As I have said, some day there will be an agreement, but for now in the desert areas, this is how one is able to live in a compatible state.

Much has been written lately about the devastating earthquakes that will be coming to the West coast. I will say that there will be harshness there for people. I do not know how to accomplish what I need to accomplish without there being some loss of life and much loss of property. However, most of the souls have this experience written in their pre-birth agreement. The agreement states … *realize that you may lose your life because the Earth needs to change some of those areas. They have become too compacted.*

EARTH MOTHER GAIA

Energies, people, layers and layers of energy... Those of you who are geologists or know geology know how the layers of these strata show different levels of history. If you think of each one of that stratum holding energy, actual patterns of what went on, you would have a better idea of what I am referring to when I say that when I rattle those layers enough it releases that energy so that it can be transmuted into the Light and resettled elsewhere.

Here perhaps is a clearer mental picture. If you travel to Israel, the land where your Master walked, there are layers of dirt on top of where he actually walked. One must dig down to find an actual footprint, if ever. It usually is not possible. Egypt is the same way, for on my planet, you see, the winds sift the soils, the rain floods the land and everything resettles. If you multiply that by centuries and realize that each one of those layers holds energy, then you may understand how an earthquake can jiggle that and allow that dark energy to rise, like dark cream to the top of a bottle so it can be siphoned off.

Therefore, I cannot apologize to the human race, but I do hold you in my heart, and it does grieve me when there is and may be even more loss of life. The cyclone in Myanmar killed many, but it is such a congested area that it needed cleansing. The earthquake in China killed many and is still doing so with the aftershocks. However, the energy of the land needed adjusting. As for the West coast of America, the same will apply. And when you have the flooding in your Midwest, it is releasing energies (*also*).

Your benevolent space brothers and sisters are helping to release this energy. They have instruments on board their ships that neutralize some of the pollution so that everything is not quite so dense. But my dear Readers, it does need to happen, for it does need to be changed. Much is going on throughout my planet. Much evil throughout my planet; much greed, the wars, all of this needs to come to a stop, needs to be resolved so that the energies can be released and

EARTH MOTHER GAIA

people of the higher consciousness can live in harmony and balance once again.

Many of you have read my articles that I have given to different channels. I have been telling humanity specifically that they need to raise their consciousness; they need to raise their vibratory rate so that I can raise mine—so that we can advance together. Those of you who do not heed the warnings that I am giving you, that God is giving you, will be displaced and not allowed to come back.

I wish to be an Eden again for the Higher Realms to come visit and to walk upon me. I wish to have a high enough vibration so that they can be sustained energetically and can take a physical body if they wish and walk among my beautiful trees and flowers and scents—the smells. Everything will be pristine; everything will be joyous. It will be an Eden. That is my goal; that is my intent and that is what I will accomplish.

Thank you, Readers, and may you continue on your path as I continue on mine. My intent is not to harm any of you. My intent is only to raise the vibrations of my body so that I may be truly a jewel in the Heavens—a jewel for God. That is all.

I am Gaia.

(*Thank you, Mother Earth, it was truly beautiful, and I hope the Readers will learn from your statements.*) You are welcome, precious child, and I know in your heart that you love me. I also know that you struggle with the Insect Kingdom. But it is your intent that I watch and your intent is pure. I would be blessed to have you continue to live with me. (*Oh thank you, thank you, Mother Gaia*)

97

CHAPTER 10- MAHATMA BUDDHA

Good morning to our Readers. I AM Yeshua. We will be starting another chapter this morning. You know we jokingly call ourselves the "Gang," but all of you Readers are becoming our Gang also. Therefore, we salute you for staying in your Light, for embracing new ideas, for allowing us to come into your hearts, for you see that is where we meet—in the heart, always in the heart.

Otherwise, it could just be your ego-personality talking to you. This Channel many times checks us out as she has stated in the previous chapters. And at times there is silence when she has asked if the Being is truly of the Light. There is silence because it was just the ego-personality wanting to take over. The silence tells her that it was just her imagination jumping the starting line, so to speak.

Consequently, it is recommended, Readers, to jot down from the previous chapters (Chapter 7) the statement that I gave to Celestial Blue Star and to use it. Use it in your own meditations, for it will quickly help you to know whether it is just ego talking or if you really have a Being making contact. So many of you have said "Oh I wish I could channel." Well, dear hearts, everyone channels. You just do not know it yet. You cannot make that differentiation between yourself fantasizing and someone actually speaking to you. By reading the statement, it will greatly help you to move forward.

Speaking of moving forward, shall we do that with a new chapter for you? We are approximately half way through our book, which is very pleasing for us. We do enjoy our time with you.

Let us bring a Presenter forward that has not spoken to

MAHATMA BUDDHA

you before and yet is part of your history. He is ancient. He has his particular following. He has his line of "religion," or spirituality. Therefore, without saying more, may I present the great Lord Mahatma Buddha.

Good morning our blessed children, **I AM** the **Mahatma**, or just plain **Buddha**. You may call me by either of those names. I come to you this morning with somewhat a heavy heart, for I see the struggle that all of you are going through. However, you are history, dear souls; you are making history.

You are living history, just as during my days when I sat under the Bodhi Tree. I did not think of myself as making, living, or being history. I merely was doing my thing. I merely was attempting to reach the final destination in spirituality, to reach that Enlightenment that all of you are seeking. It was very dear to me and somewhat amusing to me to watch my followers copy me, sitting under a Bodhi Tree, attempting to reach Enlightenment by following in my footsteps.

What people do not understand, dear souls, is that Enlightenment is unique to the beholder. Each of you in your own way is seeking Enlightenment whether you realize it or not. That is what your souls are doing by pushing aside those veils, by awakening the consciousness of your bodies. You are walking, searching, and seeking Enlightenment. To my mind, Enlightenment merely means being filled with Light, being filled with God's Light. Thus it is a unique experience for each of you.

There could be similarities but each person's path is his or her own. That is why you have heard and have been told and have read and have studied that there is a danger if you become too attached to your Master, to your guru. It would then mean you are attempting to do it his or her way. The similarity of course is that all are Light. All Light seekers are seeking more truth. All truth seekers are love; they are Light.

MAHATMA BUDDHA

The more Light you carry in your body, which you call the Light Quotient, the more love that you have become.

Love is **not** only an emotion. Some who do not understand view love as merely an emotion. What they do not realize is that **love is an energy** (*said with passion*). It is an energy that is so potent that it can move mountains! It is so potent that it can raise a person up into Enlightenment and Enlightenment is love. It is Light; it is truth; it is peace, for when you carry those attributes, there is much peace throughout your heart and energy field. When you walk your path, others bow down with reverence for you are then an Emissary of God. People cannot always make that differentiation, for they start thinking of you **as** God. But we who are doing the walking always know we are merely His Emissaries.

Now in my day (*Webster: 563-483 BC*), of course, there were slaves. However, in these modern times, one does not use that category as being a servant to someone else. I know in some of the higher echelons, one thinks of a person helping you as a servant, whereas in reality that person is there to help you, to show you different ways of being. Servants can be angels in disguise. They can be those who bring an energy that acts like a catalyst. They can be a *catalyst angel.*

People on Earth today are so divided. There are such different factions still—such groupings within groups, layers within layers. No wonder the Earth Mother is having such a difficult time. There has been much flooding and severe weather in America lately. As you have been told by Mother Gaia, that is all part of the cleansing. However, it does not make it easier when it is your house that has three feet of muddy water flowing through it.

It does not make it less traumatic. It makes it a life experience, a life experience that you have chosen. What is it like to be flooded out of your house? What was it like to see your house slide down and be demolished by a river of water, losing everything in it? What was that like for you? It

MAHATMA BUDDHA

is at times like that that people will be stretched, stretched in their belief systems, stretched in their way of looking at life. Do they blame God? Some may, but He has nothing to do with this. Many people are devastated, and it is difficult for them to realize that all of that puts them into a different frame of mind. They will have a different reference point.

They will go towards spirituality, or they will sink along with their house. Their families may be intact but where are they on their path to Enlightenment? It would behoove people to ask, *what was it my soul wanted to learn*? What is it about this devastation that I am to learn, to experience?

You see, Readers, souls who sign up for experiences such as that always are on a quest. They are questing knowledge. They are questing perhaps their own integrity, their own beliefs. Do they stand strong in their beliefs or do they see that they had made a foundation that was built on sand? When their house went floating down the river, what did that teach them? There is much to learn in these storms, in these tornadoes, devastating everything in their path.

In some ways, you see, the path of Enlightenment then is not straight and narrow and filled with bliss and roses. It winds, curves, dips down into the depths and has you climbing back up. It has you questioning: *what are you here for? What is it that you want to learn?* It has you looking at your own moral tissues (*fiber*). What is it that you need to change? Are you into possessing? (*For those flood victims*) all of those possessions have been destroyed. What is the meaning behind all of that? What was the story that your soul wanted to write?

Each of you has your own Books of Life that your soul writes into—huge books, volumes of books. Everything that you have done has been written. Each of your lifetimes is a small volume in itself that is added into your personal Library of Life. Each lifetime adds another chapter. Each lifetime is your personal storybook. Each lifetime is your personal dream or your personal nightmare. How do you confront, analyze, go forward, and step out in your dreams or nightmares? Those are lessons your soul has asked for.

People have a difficult time in accepting the fact that they are their **own** responsibility. They think that someone is telling them what to do. They think the Master Jesus is demanding this of them or that of them and they must obey him. You hear that word *obey* many times in the Christian religion.

Dear souls, the only person you would ever obey is your own I AM Self. And if you had advanced enough in your Enlightenment and God had asked something of you, you would do it gladly. But you do not think of it in terms of having to obey. You think of it only in terms of giving your heart back to God, for you are One. You are in His Heart and He is in yours.

In this modern era there are different factions of spiritual teachings. Buddhism has been categorized as a religion and people follow my teachings. Keep in mind that when I lived that lifetime and when I was teaching, I was not teaching with the thought of what people would be thinking and believing thousands of years later. I was an Oriental. I spoke to the Oriental mind. I knew no other. I saw the discrepancies, the class systems, and I was greatly grieved to think that I had lived cloistered in wealth while people outside of my gate were in poverty.

I sat under a tree until I could understand it—could understand why there was such a difference between those who had everything and those who had nothing. That understanding is *consciousness*. And I understood. I understood that there was a soul involved, and it was the soul that wanted to experience. However, souls can get caught up also. They must raise their consciousness. As you know, when you take a body you have those veils of forgetfulness. The soul would forget that it was love—that it was pure love made from the energy of love, made from the electrons of the angels of God through love. They would forget that. Therefore, they took lifetime after lifetime of poverty, trying to climb out of that. Some succeeded and some did not, for they had no one to teach them, to guide them, to lead them.

Thereby, I started teaching them the simple truths as they became known to me. Down through the ages the teachings became known as Buddhism. Just as Christianity has become distorted and is no longer pure, no longer has the pure teachings of that great Master (*Jesus*), Buddhism also has been tampered with. No religion is pure! It must be learned at the time that it is being taught, for after that you will have no longer the unadulterated truth. You will only have the scribe's conjectures. Not all scribes have a high integrity, understand. If he was tired and in order to finish a particular section, he would just stick in a word that he knew.

Readers, remember that. Religions are no longer pure. Many of your souls were there when those religions were being created. However, with your levels of consciousness at that time, you may not have believed the words spoken. You may have been in the crowds that stoned the prophets.

People, at this moment you are making history. You are part of the year 2008. With anything that goes on during this year, you are a part of history, for you are living on Earth at this time.

Enlightenment, Readers, is the most rewarding and at the same time confusing, conflicting, difficult, mind-shattering, and at times body-beaten and broken, crucified. Many of you have suffered extreme deaths. Again the soul wanted the experience. Let this lifetime, Readers, be one of joy and peace and balance. Bring peace, Light, balance, and joy into your life.

I am Mahatma Buddha. I am no longer sitting under a Bodhi tree. I am in the Light of God. I teach humanity

MAHATMA BUDDHA

from the Heavenly spheres now. I teach humanity through Channels, such as this one. I guide the energies of the world. I greet you. Greetings.

Thank you, Mahatma, it was an honor for me. You are welcome, dear child.

All right dear one that was our friend Mahatma. (That was awesome.) Yes, it was.

(*Author's note:* Mahatma, *according to Webster's Dictionary: Theosophy & Buddhism- any of a class of wise and holy persons held in special regard or reverence.*

Siddhartha Gautama *taught a philosophic system which became known as Buddhism during the 6th century B.C. in India.*

Bodhisattva *in Sanskrit means one Enlightened. Hence the Bodhi... tree.*

Yeshua *later incarnated as Mahatma Buddha.)*

CHAPTER 11- LADY GUINEVERE- CAMELOT

Good morning to all of our Readers and to this Channel. We are back once again. It is always such a joy for us to come to you. I hope you realize that. As this Channel sits here in preparation for us to come forth and she is speaking and thinking of us with gratitude, we come to her. We hope you Readers know what a privilege it is. That is the way she puts it, "Do you know what a privilege it is to have these tremendous Light Beings come forth?"

We want to say that it is a privilege for us also, dear Readers; it is a privilege for us also to speak our thoughts and to have you hold the books and read the thoughts and enjoy them. One of the Readers wrote in an e-mail to this Channel that she learned more through our books than she had learned going to all the different churches for many years and sitting and listening to the various sermons. What a joy for us to hear; what a joy.

We have another surprise for you. Actually, we think that each Presenter that comes forth is a wonderful surprise for you. Most have not spoken to this Channel before for this book will have different information, you see. It is a woman this time. We need women speaking to you, do we not? I will let her introduce herself, so I will step aside now.

Oh what a glorious morning it is here in Arizona. I have been in different parts of your country and have watched as the people have struggled as the Earth Mother goes through her changes—one being the inundation of water over the Plains. **I AM** known as **Lady Guinevere**, the **Lady of Camelot**. There has been much myth written about me, but I am real. I lived. I wrote my story just as all of you are writing yours. I carry much love so I am known as the **Lady of Love**

LADY GUINEVERE- CAMELOT

(**Queen of Hearts**). Of course your Mother Mary also carries love. Each of us carries a strong (*dominate*) attribute, shall we say, and mine is Love.

History has me as a lover of Sir Lancelot and as a wife to King Arthur. That is true. Sir Lancelot is my Flame. He is the other half of me. Therefore, when he came into my life, he came with a purpose and we were drawn to each other as two moths to a flame! This was set up before we were born. There were lessons to be taught and lessons to be learned by all who played the game.

In modern times people think of me as having sinned, and I must say it was not taken too kindly by the populace in those days either. It was thought of as court intrigues, but it went more deeply than that—the dynamic was much deeper. We carried coding that was dispersed. We held each other and I truly loved two men. King Arthur played the Father-figure in my life—Sir Lancelot, the dashing, younger lover. We were then, you see, a triangle, a triangle of energy that has expanded over time.

People of modern generation do not realize that those stories that are somewhat mythological have kernels of truth in them. They have a purpose and a deeper meaning. It was somewhat touching to me when your President John Kennedy and his beautiful wife Jacquelyn lived in the White House. There was much feminine energy and games being played out. Mrs. Kennedy referred to their life there as Camelot, for in many ways it was magical. She played her part; she played her part.

What do I have to teach you today? Many times when one travels through history, one can pick up a thread and find that not much has changed. It was the same as in my day. We had a fairytale kind of life. We had knights who spent hours shining their armor, practicing on their horses. They held such a passion in those days, going out on quests—quests of the heart—carrying banners for God. In their quests many times, they would be drawn off their path. They would take wrong turns in consciousness.

It is the same today. Many people start out in their life's work with such passion for what they will do. Then when they are actually in that office, they are drawn off their path. This happens so many times during your presidencies, America. The dark forces try their utmost to influence anything of the Light.

Therefore, dearest Readers, the point I am making is that there is a part of you, the soul part, which has such joy and a tremendous yearning to be successful. There is such joy and it jumps into life thinking, *I will do this and I will do that*. And then life starts to shade and shape him or her. It puts a film over those ambitions and he finds that he loses his enthusiasm for he always finds that someone is better at something than he is.

These souls start giving over their power. They start giving over their truth for another's truth. They start giving over their way of looking at the world for someone else's way. Then when they hit middle age—in what you call the 40's crises—they find that they have made a rut for themselves with a huge fence in the rut. They are sitting on that fence afraid to jump one way or another—afraid to make any changes. They are afraid to make any changes in their jobs, where they are going to live, what they accept as a new idea. They become stuck.

The doors start to close. The doors of opportunity start to close, for the *Law of Attraction* has never stopped its impetus. They are now drawing ill health to themselves; they are drawing boredom to themselves; they are drawing addictions to themselves; they are drawing lack to themselves—lack in all ways. What started out as a beautiful life became tainted. They took upon distorted religions, distorted politics, and distorted professions.

LADY GUINEVERE- CAMELOT

They got into debt. They became possessed by their possessions. So many times you have heard the phrase, *men and their toys.* Many men will not give up their toys even though they no longer can afford them, even though they are sinking in debt, borrowing, giving promissory notes to their spouses or friends. They refuse to change their ways. Their way of the good life has now become a burden, a millstone around their neck, and they are drowning with it.

Of course there is a constant battle with the mind and ego that wants to keep the status quo and refuses to look at reality and to make any changes for the better. That is not Camelot. That is a fairytale gone badly. So many people create Camelot in their minds, but they do not know how to keep the story real for they are afraid of change.

This day, the 16th of June, is a propitious day for it is a Master energy number—June being the 6th month and this being the 16th day. When the Masters are working with the energies for humanity, there is a portal that is opened for that particular day. The Masters come and work with you, if you will sit and allow that energy to come forth. Energy of joy and harmony will awaken the joy and harmony in your hearts. (*Each month holds different Master energies.*)

This Channel recently listened to a CD by the group that calls themselves *Abraham,* channeled by Esther Hicks. Abraham was saying that the soul must figure it out. Do not keep saving a person, figuring out his problems for him. Let the soul figure it out. Give the person the room to figure it out. In some ways it becomes a *sink or swim mentality,* for how can a soul grow if there is someone always telling it the way to do something?

Camelot... Camelot is one of magic, the ability to lead, the ability to hear one's own soul, the ability to bring joy and harmony into one's life. Yes, there can be a magical component to life, for is it not magic when the soul and God are in agreement? Is it not magic when your life holds such

110

LADY GUINEVERE- CAMELOT

peace and love for humanity and tranquility and joy (*said with great emotion*)? Is that not magic? Does that not make your life Camelot? Each person has a Camelot in his or her own heart. It is up to you to hold steady to that, to strive for that.

Do you think that God sends you to Earth just so you can be in dire predicaments and dire circumstances? Do you not think that God sends you to Earth to experience joy, harmony, and peace so that He too might experience that? Do you not think that He gets rather tired of always experiencing the conflict through you? Where is your harmony? Where is your Camelot in life? Each life holds a magical spot for you—your personal Camelot. It is up to you to find the path there, to figure it out, as the Abraham group said. Figure out how to get there.

As the knights of old went out on their quests, was it not the quest itself that brought the excitement—the hope and the prayers that they would find the Holy Grail? Was that not the excitement in the quest?

Your lifetime, dear souls, is meant to be a quest, is meant to find your personal Camelot. It must be so for consciousness will bring you to that place where you will know at last what love is all about. You will know that you are love; God is love. You will know. I invite each one of you to find the Camelot that is within you, for you are love. When one quests for his or her love to come, for your Sir Lancelot to come, for your Lady Guinevere to come, it will happen. The magic is in your heart. Go on your personal quest and find **your** Camelot.

I AM Lady Guinevere.

(*Thank you, Lady; it is truly a beautiful chapter.*) You are welcome, precious Channel; you are welcome.

(*Author's note: for definitive information of Lady Guinevere and the archetype of Camelot go to Michelle*

111

*Eloff's website www.thelightweaver.org and **2:2 Re-Union of Love through the Sacred Self, Activation, 01-25-08.**)*

CHAPTER 12- ARCHANGEL METATRON

Good morning, precious Readers, I AM Yeshua back to bring you another chapter. The book is half finished now. At the time that we start a book, this Channel is always somewhat nervous for she does not know which direction the work is going to go. But now she realizes that this book is to give various Masters the opportunity to come forth and to give you their teachings. As you well know, we have male and female energy nicely disbursed throughout the pages. There needs always to be a balance, you see.

Keep a balance in everything that you do, using your masculine and feminine principles. In that way you are practicing androgyny, for in the higher spheres that is what we are. We are androgynous. However, when we wish to we can present a more masculine image or a more feminine image if that is the woman's wish. Therefore, we still use your English pronouns for distinction.

*We have a great Being coming this morning, the world's greatest Archangel. He is the Archangel of Light, of the electrons. You have heard of the fabrication of time. He spins the fabrication of Light throughout the Universes. His name is the **Archangel** and **Lord Metatron**.*

Good morning, I AM He. I am the Being you know as **Archangel Metatron**. Some of you Readers may not realize that I come many times to different Channels and teach. Do not have me floating around in the Heavens, more or less just keeping an eye on humanity. You have that saying *to roll up your sleeves and to get into the nitty-gritty of it all.* Therefore, I come today to give you a lesson. It is a lesson on receiving your Light. So many people are not that conscious of the fact that they are indeed unraveling those codes of Light that reside in each of their chakras. Unravel your Light and let it shine forth, Readers. You have coding throughout your body that holds Light.

It would be similar to turning on the light bulbs throughout your body and the light switch is within each chakra. Flip it on and let your Light shine. For when you have light does it not dissipate any shadow? If you go into a room without light, is it not dark? And when you turn your electric light switch on does not the dark dissipate?

In this analogy this is what you as Light workers, Light weavers, Light Beings are doing when you are walking the Earth in your full Light garment. How can there be darkness around you when you are Light? You come into a room and you light it up. You walk down the street and everyone you pass is affected by your Light. It permeates them and goes into their dark areas and helps them light up.

Many times someone else has a dark closet and by your simply passing him by, or talking to him, or by shaking hands, or having lunch in a restaurant, your Light permeates his dark closet. Now what does that mean to you in a more practical sense? What do people keep in their closets? Some have old clothes; some have memory books; some keep dark secrets—it is the place to keep your dark secrets. In humanity there is the Internet and there are different Internet sites that one can go to that hold dark energy. I am referring to the pornographic trade through the Internet. Is that not dark? I am speaking of the dating-game with the children of God that are not of age. Children have much curiosity. They do not realize they are being caught in a web. They find it exciting and they start to fantasize. Before they know it, they have fantasized the fact that they are speaking to a loving father figure or even a mother figure. They then get pulled into the web. The dark pictures start flying back and forth over the lines.

This can happen even in families of Light. Many times people bring in children (*birth them*) for the express purpose of helping them to awaken to their Light, helping them to find their Light switch, but they are not always successful. Many times the children must reach a more mature age before they can hear any wisdom.

Many of the youths join Christian churches. Now is that a bad thing? If it keeps them on a positive path, it can be a good thing. It can help children. Then when they grow up, they will need to be de-programmed (*said with a smile*), for much that they have heard will not have been truth. And yet there is much truth in what your Lord Jesus said if the scribes wrote it correctly. He followed those commandments, but he had his own interpretation that was closer to the truth than what was being taught by the rabbis. It caused great dissention among the people. They did not understand him.

How many of you in your own families are understood? In this Channel's family it is known as *Mom's World*. Her children and grandchildren do not enter into *Mom's World* very often. It is only when she gives them her latest books that they may thumb through them, but none of them have read them from cover to cover. What does she do about it? She stays in her Light. It saddens her but as the saying goes, she lets them *figure it out*. She is there for them any time they wish to bring their troubles to her, but she does not press upon them her beliefs of her world.

Light is two-faced, for Light is love. You cannot have one without the other. If there is not love with your Light, then it is not of the higher level of love. Love is energy, as you have been told. It has many levels to it.

You can think of Light as a pure diamond. You can think of love as a pure diamond. However, even in diamonds there can be specks of charcoal. There are different gradations of the stone. There are different gradations of love. You have been told before that the lower levels of love are of the ego. The person gets into lust, into control, into possession.

ARCHANGEL METATRON

So many times in your movies you have seen it portrayed where mothers and fathers cannot let their children go. They hold the children to them with such a heavy hand. They possess them, trying to mold them into an exact replica of what and who they as parents are. You bring your children into the world for many reasons. Many times it is a karmic tie between you. There have been the pre-birth agreements. However, you are helping each other; you are teaching each other.

Some people are apt to think that a little two-year-old body could not be teaching the adult anything. But that soul is. It might be teaching the parents *patience, love in different degrees, protectiveness, caring, compassion, joy, a willingness to share, a willingness to give, a willingness to think of someone else besides you.* It lights up your narcissism; it lights up your dark closets.

Light is deceptive. People have a different perception of what Light is. It is energy; it is electrons that can penetrate and travel swiftly. You have that saying that something *travels at the speed of light.* Light travels. Therefore, as we have said before, when you walk down the street, your Light is traveling. It is emanating out from you, touching everything in its path. It touches the animals; it touches the Deva world, the fairies that are going about their business of tending to the beautiful plants and flowers. You could walk through a field of wild flowers, and if you are of the Light, the flowers would take much joy with your presence.

Broaden your horizon, people; think of Light in an expansive way. Think of it as permeating everything. It permeates everything! When you are in your Light, you could sit next to someone who is in a shadow-mode and just by your presence your Light can lift that shadow; or it will light up what is causing that shadow. It will light up that person's hidden closet. Nothing is to remain secret from now on.

ARCHANGEL METATRON

The energy coming onto the planet will reveal everything in people's closets, for the energy is Light and Love from the Creator. It is multi-Rays and colors—each one with a specific purpose. Whenever you hear of people being caught in misdeeds, cheating, cheating the public, or caught in their sexual games, their dark side opened and aired for everyone to see, that is the (*effect of this*) energy; that is the Light that is probing into the dark areas of that person.

As you hold this book in your hands, there is much Light in it. People feel the energy in books. They pick them up and hold them; they re-read them for the energy as well as the wisdom that they hold. As I look at humanity, I am delighted to see the Light shining ever more brightly. People are turning their Light on in their closets. Now it might be a dim wattage, but there is still a Light where there was not one before.

Look at your own secret closets, people. What is it that needs to come out? What is it that you need to let go of? Look around your environment, your own house. How much of it is really something that you could not do without? What can you let go of? Let your Light shine in every corner of your house. Let the Light shine in every corner of your body, which is the soul's house. Let it shine.

I come to Earth to help humanity. I shine my Light on humanity. I AM Light. I AM Love. Take me into your hearts for there is where you keep your darkest secrets—the dark side of your soul. Love and Light are one. Light and Love are one. Know that all you have to do is set the intention that you are turning on your light switch in every chakra so that your Light shines like a beacon to the outside world. When you walk the path, people who you encounter will feel your Light and know that your Light will awaken in them the idea that they too are Light and Love.

I AM Archangel Metatron and it has been my greatest pleasure to come and offer you my Light.

ARCHANGEL METATRON

Greetings. (*Thank you, Lord*)

All right, dear one, that's it for today. Until we meet again, adieu. (Adieu)

CHAPTER 13- SENATOR BARACK OBAMA

6-26-08 Dearest ones, this Channel has been sitting here for over a half hour contemplating what is it about the energy of your Senator Barack Obama and his wife Michelle that has people seeing him as one of the dark, has people taking an instant dislike to him, has people judging him? If people act as mirrors for you... But dear souls, what I wish to tell you is that in the country of America, and actually in other countries, there are people who sincerely wish that Obama and his family would disappear—would drop dead, using a more slang phrase.

It is this (outside) energy that (surrounds him) that keeps people from seeing his Light. Let me give you an example. Many times one can pick up a piece of fine jewelry, or shall we say, a cup. The cup is so covered with years of dirt and muck (from the environment) that the inscriptions and the engravings on the cup are barely discernable. Therefore, the owner of the cup, perhaps a new owner, starts to clean the cup and now he can read the inscriptions and can see the beauty that shines forth. If the cup is gold or silver, the shine almost can be blinding.

This is what has happened in a similar fashion to that blessed family. It is mud being thrown on a glass window. It is mud being thrown on a silver or gold chalice. Until that mud, that dark energy (which is not his) is washed away, the true Light of the Being and the wife and family is not discernable. Some refuse to see his Light because he has a middle name that they feel is evil. They feel that it is Islamic and therefore it must represent a dark nature. People, this is such third-dimensional thinking. We cannot convince you to think otherwise, but I ask you all who are pondering this to break through this sludge that is surrounding this blessed family. Let his Light shine through. The days ahead are dark

SENATOR BARACK OBAMA

indeed for America. As the days approach more closely to the actual election in November, the dark will rally their forces and attack even more.

We are taking the time this morning to speak about this for it is becoming quite a controversial subject. You cannot have it both ways, America. And one of the problems, of course, is the Fundamentalists in Christianity! The Christians are adding to this. It is their energy—the negative righteousness, their erroneous belief systems and thoughts that only they have the answers.

Do you honestly believe, Christian Fundamentalists, that I, Yeshua-Jesus-Sananda, would be that lop-sided in my heart? Do you honestly believe that I would not embrace this family of Light—this family that is from a noble lineage and far greater than you have any idea, far greater than you have any notion of? Oh people, I do not know if this book will be out in time for the elections. We of course cannot make you see through to the Light.

However, if Senator Obama is elected, there will be such joyous singing in the Heavens, for it means that America will be pulled forward, will be pulled up and out of the gutter that the present Administration has put her in. She has lost her respect in foreign countries. Everything about America has dwindled—everything that was good has dwindled. With a new Administration led by Senator Obama, and hopefully President Barack Obama, America will begin to make her long comeback. Now will he be able to make enough changes so that the sliding path that America is on can be turned around? Again, you see, it depends upon the people who are around him. Will Americans allow him to do his job? Or will the heavy prejudice... Will Americans just allow him to put forth his new ideas on change?

It will be a very tight race, for there are enough people who are against Senator Obama who will either not vote or

SENATOR BARACK OBAMA

they will vote for someone else. All I can say is if you only knew what we know; if you only could see what we see.

I now wish to bring in another Presenter and let this be a political chapter—Chapter 13. He will introduce himself. (Thank you, Yeshua)

Good morning everyone, **I AM Ashtar**, the next Presenter. (*Ashtar, I need to check you out.* By all means! *I now demand in the name of Jesus the Christ...* Yes, I AM Ashtar.) Things are heating up for America. I come this morning with somewhat a heavy heart for I recently have been channeling information through Susan Leland* telling about the death of Tim Russert—how it was not a natural death, but one instigated by the dark side to create a heart attack. It worked. His body could not fight off the negative influences, and he succumbed to the pressures leaving behind a legacy, one of truth, and a legacy that reporters will strive for. They will not believe any of this (*about his death being one of murder*) nor will they think it.

However, some find it somewhat strange. You have a perfect example of someone who was in vibrant health. And yes, he had some heart problems, as most of America does, but the dark energies prevailed. It was with the permission of the soul that we allowed it to happen. Could we have neutralized that energy that was used? YES, but Mr. Russert at the time... (*At this point, the transmission was interrupted.*)

6-27-08 *Good morning, dearest one, the Gang's all here. We had a bit of a problem yesterday when the transmission was interrupted by a client that needs your help. So shall we just continue where we left off? Ashtar was speaking with you. He is standing here and we will open the door so that he may come forth once again.*

Here I am, back once again. **I AM Ashtar**. I was speaking to you yesterday of the fact that one of your greatest reporters, Tim Russert, was murdered. Not in the way that most people

SENATOR BARACK OBAMA

would think with a bullet, but in a way that one could call supernatural, where energy was shot into the heart causing a fatal heart attack. This happened when he was on the set. The dark Beings in another dimension (so that they could not be seen) used technology to literally stop his Light. However, that dear man is on our side now. He is with us on the ships and he is helping us by pinpointing the discrepancies of the different political factions. There were games afoot, games that were not of the Light. He knew many secrets, and he was not afraid to tell the world about what he had discovered. It was this information that was being kept from the world by the dark forces.

You have been told I am sure, if not in these books but perhaps from others, that the energy coming from the Creator is of such potent ingredients that this energy simply lets the cats out of the bags. It opens the doors, doors that were locked. It opens the secret closets. No one on the planet will be able to keep a secret for long. Something or someone will let that secret out.

The dark forces that killed Mr. Russert thought that they could put a cap on this information, but you will find that other reporters who have similar information will start speaking out. There are several reporters of high integrity who will loosen their hold on keeping political secrets and will let them out. It is time, Readers; it is time for humanity to know what is going on in your world and especially in the United States. It is not a pretty picture.

The present Administration has brought great dishonor to this country. This country was started by the will of men to have freedom. It was blessed by God. It was orchestrated by Saint Germain and other highly Lighted Beings. The Signers of the Declaration were prodded by the Light Beings on the other side. Those Signers of the Declaration had come in for this lifetime. It was their job description, but as you know, you do not always remember your spiritual job description. You are apt to be caught up in the different factions, the various opinions of people. That is similar to what is happening today.

Presently in June 2008, your Senator Barack Obama is the Democratic nominee-to-be. He will be officially sworn into that at the Democratic convention. **I reiterate: I, Ashtar of the Federation of Light of the Galactic Command, hereby say with passion that Senator Barack Obama is a Light filled Being as is his wife, Michelle, as are his two little girls. They may be little in age and stature but they are very powerful new age Light Beings, diamond-children that he and Michelle have brought in. This is a Light-filled family. It is blessed by God.**

One could even call this family a Holy family. Now I know this will not go over well with many Fundamentalists, but Holy means blessed by God. People are not allowing him, accepting him to be fully into his purpose. He has run a fairly clean campaign. People have given him millions of dollars for his campaign. However, the opposite candidate repeatedly slung mud at him. There are many in the opposite factions who are still not accepting of him.

It is not purely one of racism, although there is some racism in there. It is simply that people who do not embrace his ideology do not embrace him as a learned man of integrity. They cannot accept that he could and will, if given the chance lead them, lead them to higher ground, and lead them to prosperity once again. He will bring balance to America. However, the opposite factions on the political arena do not see that.

Most of the people who are following Senator Hillary Clinton and the former President Bill Clinton do not know they are Illuminati. They would not even accept that thought. We shall say no more, but if America does not wake up so that they may see through the mud-slinging, so that they can polish off the sludge that has collected around Senator

SENATOR BARACK OBAMA

Obama, if they do not wake up, they will lose an opportunity to regain freedom.

That is freedom in every sense of the way from the First Amendment—so much of that has been taken away from them. All of this terrorist-attacking jargon is nothing but rhetoric filled with fear. It has no place in America. Terrorism was barely a known factor before the government conspiracy of 9/11. Ever since then, terrorism and war from the warmongers has been publicized by the media of which many knew no better.

America, dear friends, is a land of beauty. It is a land of opportunity; it is a land of Love Thy Neighbor; it is a land of abundance. Dear friends, let it prosper again; let it become the jewel of the world that it was meant to be. America has always had the reputation of being a country where one could have freedom of speech, could prosper and yes, could even become president. America is made up of people from all over the world, speaking various languages and dialects, dressing in different clothes, living their own lifestyles within the lifestyle of America, within safety. However, it has only been in recent years that America has lost its ideals; it has lost its morality.

When you remove God from plaques and schools and buildings, you are removing the Energy of God. That is never a good thing, people—never a good thing. He must stand back and let free will have full reign. Therefore, He can no longer protect those areas where His name is not honored. It is your free will; it is your free will.

Thereby, what is the will of the people now? They are divided; they are divided. Some are just sitting on the fence and they call themselves Independents, embracing neither Republicans nor Democrats. That is certainly their prerogative also; that is their free will.

SENATOR BARACK OBAMA

America, where art thou, America? I AM Ashtar and I bless you this day.

(Thank you, Ashtar, it was potent!) You are welcome, dear Channel, you are welcome.

*Susan Leland channels Ashtar. Find her at: www. ashtarontheroad.com/catalog/item/2497194/2108034.

CHAPTER 14- LORD ENOCH- CHANGE

Good morning everyone, we are back once again after a few days off. This Channel is feeling somewhat nostalgic this morning, for tomorrow will be the Fourth of July for America. She looks back on her childhood and all the various 4ᵗʰ of July celebrations, sparklers that twinkled and stung just a bit as the sparks touched your skin, the tradition of waiting until nightfall, having watermelon—so many traditions for America. And yet this date for 2008 is probably at one of the lowest points that it has ever been.

However, dear friends, everything must change. It is in that wonderful book by God where He said that the **only constant is** change. That is somewhat of a dichotomy, is it not? The only thing that is constant in your Universe is the fact that everything changes. Every cell in your body changes, and as your body grows, you change—your brain changes, your chakras change.*

Everything changes. Some people change more than others. What makes that so? Is it because they are more adventurous? Is it because they are more willing to change? Is it because they are more willing to let certain belief systems drop by the wayside—those belief systems that no longer serve them?

This morning we are going to have a new speaker, and it will be interesting for all of us to hear what he is going to say. He has never come before, but he is very ancient. Therefore, it gives us the greatest privilege to step aside and let this great Lord of the Heavens speak.

I am your next Presenter. **I AM** known as **Enoch,** Enoch of those ancient days, Enoch of those biblical times, Enoch who brought much information to his scribe, J.J. Hurtak,

LORD ENOCH- CHANGE

Ph.D., as we wrote the Keys, the *Keys of Enoch*, which some refer to as their personal bible.

What does it mean when we speak of *keys*? Keys unlock different concepts; keys unlock different apparatus; keys unlock codings that reside in your body; keys unlock many of the wonders of your world in physics, biology, aerodynamics, and space dynamics. In your everyday lives, keys are used to unlock some perception, some energy that will bring forth a new revelation.

Not everyone understands another person's key. Not everyone will understand what that particular person's key is for. Keys can be private, for they are codes—they are codes to another world, to another Universe. They are codes that unlock the mysteries of the Creator. (*Keys are either physically solid or are symbolic—metaphors.*)

Much of humanity today does not think in those terms, does not think of themselves as being full of codes that need to be unlocked. They think they are just flesh and blood. They do not realize that they have thousands and thousands of codes within them (*said with great passion*)—thousands of codes stored in their body's memories, many residing in the base chakra, the chakra that tells their life's story.

The soul brings these codes in when it is building its body; it puts in this codification. There are codes in the brain that rewire and connect to the different glandular systems—the pineal, pituitary, thymus, hypothalamus—all glands that affect the brain. It is the brain that affects your third eye, your chakra that can send (*the spiritual*) you into outer space. It is not known to humanity that many of the secrets of the Universe are held in the chakras of the human body. Scientists look through telescopes to read the stars; they look through microscopes to read the body. However, those instruments are not capable of delving into the chakras where the hidden codified information is held.

LORD ENOCH- CHANGE

One day this may be so. Someday a master teacher will come into a physical body, maybe another Einstein. He will come into a body and he will be able to develop an instrument that can read the codification that is held in the chakras. This is technology that is way beyond what humanity knows at this point. Much of humanity does not even recognize the fact that it has chakra points (*chuckles*). There is so much yet that humanity does not understand.

Yeshua was saying at the beginning of the chapter that God had said that the only one constant was *change*. And yet that seems to be the most difficult for people. Is that not quite ironic? The one thing that one can count on, absolutely count on is *change*! Everything changes.

When I came this morning, I did not have a particular set topic. I had not been near enough to this Channel before, so I was not sure what she would be open to. However, I find that she is an open vessel; she is able to handle change. And she does it with a swiftness that belies her senior years. Therefore, I will keep that theme of *change* and will make that the title of this chapter.

I will tell you of some of the changes that I see happening on the horizon and into the future. Remember when any subject is considered for the future, that subject is likely to change, simply because of man/woman's free will.

One of the greatest changes that you are already experiencing is the change in the weather. Arizona has had over twenty straight days of the temperature above 110 degrees. This will continue. There may be days where the temperature may dip one or two degrees, but the higher degrees will continue. Then the rains of the monsoons will bring a short-lived cooling down period. Therefore, that is one of the changes—a steady trend of hot days in Arizona.

Another change will be in your season of the hurricanes. There will not be as many as previously feared, but those that do come will have strong winds and be devastating in their path. Category 5 hurricanes are on the horizon.

This Channel wrote a previous book and one of the chapters was entitled, *California Burning. (Your Space Brothers and Sisters Greet You, Chapter 11.)* It seems as if now there is a sequel, for California fires are burning once again. This will continue to plague California throughout the season. Some of it will be carelessness of the people and some fires will be from lightening strikes.**

There are volcanoes that are just biding their time. They will be spewing forth their ashes—not just one going off, but several at the same time, for they trigger each other. It is the same with earthquakes. The entire West coast of America ought to be under an earthquake and volcano alert. The fact that the schools are closed for the summer is good, but that danger will continue for quite some time.

In the previous chapter, the theme was about Senator Obama and the coming election for America. One way or another, this will bring a change in the administration even if your favorite candidate is not elected. The whole procedure still will bring about change, for not one of those candidates will do exactly the same thing that the previous administration did. Each candidate will bring his change. It will also matter greatly what vice president they will choose.

Changes are political; changes are natural acts of Nature; changes are natural acts of Mother Earth. Then you will have the changes of each person's body on this planet. Changes will be in the chakra systems that affect everyone's energy fields. The bodies will be vibrating at a higher rate. The children that are being born vibrate at a higher level than their parents do.

If Mother Earth is going to raise her vibratory rate, the newer generations must also have a higher vibration. Therefore, each of the new babies being born is vibrating at

LORD ENOCH- CHANGE

a higher frequency than their parents and teachers. This will cause many problems in the schools until they start changing their curriculums and stop trying to teach them in the way they did fifty years ago, or even 25 years ago. It must be changed.

The children are brighter. They come in with more wisdom. Most of them will not understand their parents or teachers, for they come in with a purpose. They will be very strong in their ideas and reactions to their environment. The children will be more positive and they will be more aware of the ecosystem; they will be more aware of what is required for a greener world.

There will be changes in the entire space organization. There will be a purge. They will see where many dollars are being wasted on ideas that are more fantasy than actuality. There will be changes in engineering so that your modes of transportation will be more productive. Your modes of air travel will be swifter. Your airports will be revamped. The security systems will be done away with. They were foolish to begin with. People will be able to keep their shoes on. The long security lines will disappear.

There will be a new energy fuel system so that airplanes can fly the skies once again without going into bankruptcy. Just as everything has been taken away as far as an air flight is concerned, even having to pay for your baggage as of now, it will all start to come back—one air- line after another, like a domino effect. You will have beautiful catered meals once again so that the flyer joyously anticipates what will be served. The food will be more gourmet and soft drinks will no longer have to be purchased.

You will have shuttles that will take you to space- ships and you will have travel to off-worlds. Of course this is several hundreds of years from now. However, we are speaking of changes in history. When this generation dies and then comes back once again, they could find that all of these predicted

LORD ENOCH- CHANGE

changes have happened. Everything changes. It changes in my world. It changes in my world where all is energy, love, and Light. Everything is changing. We are all evolving still. I now know things way beyond what I knew when I first wrote *The Keys of Enoch*. However, no one is ready to absorb the material yet. Many are unable to absorb the first book. That wonderful channel, Dr. Hurtak, did a magnificent job with our book.

Therefore, Readers, I hope I have given you a peek at what you can expect—a peek into the present and the future, all of which are still changing. Remember that everything changes. Everything is influenced by the free will of others, by the energies that are flowing forth. Everything is changing because everything is connected. You cannot have one change in South Africa without there being a similar change in America. In that sense, the world is small because it is your world and everything and everybody in that world is connected. Therefore, it is one world, one microcosm, for the biggest macrocosm is within you. It is your inner world that is the largest world of all.

It has been my pleasure and I thank you for your time. I AM Enoch.

(Thank you, Lord, do you and I have a particular connection?) Of course we are connected. Anyone who had biblical experiences such as you and others have had would be connected to the ancient prophets of old. Those prophets, some of which you know in present bodies, were also connected with you. Many of your Readers are connected with you and therefore are connected with the prophets and therefore are connected with me, Enoch. I come to many and it is my pleasure to do so. I leave you now and I bless you. *(Thank you, Lord)*

All right dear soul that was our friend Enoch, a pleasant surprise for you speaking on changes. (Yes). Type that up

*and we will be with you in a couple of days. Blessings, dear
one.*

(*And Then God Said...Then I Said...And Then He
Said, Chapter 2, Volume One *by Celestial Blue Star of the
Pleiades, David of Arcturus, and Suzanne (Suzy) Ward. www.
awakenedhearts.com/books2.htm).*

*(**www.matthewbooks.com. July 4, 2008.)*

CHAPTER 15- REFLECTIONS of a FEW

*Good morning Readers, the Gang is all here. We are going to be speaking this morning on a different subject, one that is always dear to my heart. **I AM Yeshua** and with me is my counterpart, my adored wife, Mary Magdalene. If you go up the ladder, there is Sananda with the Lady Nada.*

This morning let us bring those members forth. They are all a part of me. Let us bring them and see what they have to say. So for now I will make room, and we will see what happens.

Hello, blessed children of my heart, **I AM Mary Magdalene**, Goddess in my own right, Lady Master in my own right. My fellow sisters and I are working feverishly to help humanity connect with their Divine feminine. It is somewhat humorous to us to see the male bodies struggle when they are told that they need to connect with the Divine feminine.

The fallacies of your sexuality have permeated so deeply the structures of people's belief systems. They mix it all up with *oh, I can't admit I have a feminine side; they'll think that I am a homosexual.* Those who are strong in their spirituality will know we are speaking of energy. We are speaking of balance, aren't we—the balance between masculine and feminine energies?

We have talked about this before, but the majority of humanity is not ready for this information. It might seep into them eventually, but they are not ready for it yet. This Channel's own family has male members, especially in the extended families, who would think that she truly is an *odd ball* if she dared say to them, *what side are you coming from, your Divine feminine or your masculine energy?* They would

135

not even know what she is talking about (*chuckles*). Isn't that the way it is with most of humanity?

People do not realize just how important it is to have a balance of those energies. They cannot advance up that ladder of evolution unless they have a balance of those energies. They stay at the same level, following the pugilistic sports. Or if they followed the feminine sport of say, ice skating, people will immediately think that a male skater is using too much of his feminine side. *He must be a homosexual.*

Eventually, all of that type of third dimensional thinking will recede. It will dissipate. Go to your hearts, dear people. Listen to your heart; listen to your soul; what is your soul saying? It is difficult for those who embrace the violent sports to think in terms of a feminine consciousness being a part of them that lies fallow in the subconscious. They do not want to touch it with a ten-foot pole, for they are afraid of the whole concept. One of these days they will not be so afraid. When they get to the other side, to Heaven, to Nirvana, or whatever name they call that dimension, they will get some enlightenment on the subject. However, it will be up to the soul to bring that information back into its next body, would it not?

The energies are changing on your planet. They are coming in with such force and swiftness that many people are finding they are having a hard time keeping up. They will sleep more; they will eat differently, have different types of food cravings. You may wish to have an egg salad on a cracker in the middle of the morning. You may wish to have a succulent strawberry, or two or three, before going to bed. The cravings will be different for everyone. That is true, but allow them to be, and if they are not harmful for you in any way, listen to your body and let it have those mini-snacks versus perhaps one or two large meals. Be willing to change. That is all that is required—to be willing to change and follow your soul and listen to your body.

REFLECTIONS of a FEW

Each month holds a different vibration for you. Learn to have your *still time* so that you can partake of this energy, even if you do not know what it is all about. Simply sit and ask for clarification; ask to be part of the energy for that month; ask to be connected to the Goddess or the Master for that month. All you need to do is ask; you do not always need to know the particulars about something. However, it is good if you can, but not everyone has an Internet (*from which to gather the information*); not everyone has the ability to receive different transmissions. Therefore, accept and just know that all you have to do is to set the intention and let your angels work with you.

I am going to step aside now and let a fellow Teacher come forth. Blessings to all of you Readers, I enjoy my times with you. I AM Mary Magdalene. (*Thank you, Mary.*) You are welcome.

I am the next one in line. I am known as **Sananda.** It is with the greatest pleasure that I come to you this morning. Times are difficult for you, America. How many of you are ready to swim with the changes? How many of you are ready to go forward—to embrace the changes and to know that your soul has this plan for you? Now will there be changes in the plans? There could be; you could re-negotiate your contracts, but keep in mind that all that is required of you is flexibility—to be flexible. Be flexible in your body; be flexible in your thinking; be flexible with any change that comes your way.

You could make several changes each day if you were willing to do so. Do you not know that if you refuse to change that you are stopping the energy from flowing correctly into your body? Do you know that your chakras are changing constantly at a more rapid rate? Do you know that if you do not accept the fact that you can change and be flexible that this actually stops the energy from advancing you to higher levels of consciousness?

REFLECTIONS of a FEW

How does one reach a higher level of consciousness? You do so by being flexible, by coming to a reality from a child's perception, being joyous in what is coming for you each day. What will happen today? What new change will I see today? What new change will I implement today? How much fun! *Thank you Father for this most adventurous life, thank you!* Be appreciative.

Be in forgiveness. How many of you forget to forgive— almost on a daily basis? Forgive the fact that just maybe you were not always correct in your choices. Forgive yourself. That does not mean you cannot change your choice. That is what change is all about. That is what choices are all about. They are made to be changed. The great Lord Enoch just spoke on change and how everything is going to change.

As I see it, or we see it because as you know we have quite a few Beings with us, one of the biggest hurdles is to change your belief systems about your religions, dear souls. When you think of me—Yeshua/Jesus/Sananda—when you think of the aspects of me, how many of you immediately picture me on the cross? Can one ever divorce from that picture of Jesus hanging on the cross? It is not true, Readers; it is not true (*said with strong emotion*).

All the stories of the puncture wounds of the hands, feet and side are not true. Those are images brought from the third dimension. Remember Book FOUR where we wrote on *Realities...* It was a different reality. It never happened. **It never happened!** This hurdle of believing what you have been programmed to believe by various religions will be a hard jump to make for most of humanity.

The religions were not even started in truth. Their foundation was not built on truth. There are even questionable teachings about the Commandments and Moses' part in all of that. Was Moses just one Being? No, he was not. There were threads of several of us Masters in Moses.* One person cannot bring in the Laws for humanity and do it all on his own.

It is not possible. The energy is such that it is not possible. Therefore, make the intention as you are reading this chapter, say to yourself, *my intention this day is to change my belief structure about religion.* Now you may not really know how you are going to change it, but the fact that you are willing to change is the first step. Let it go; do not make any statement or buy into another (*religious*) belief—simply let it go. Let it rest in the hands of God as spirituality.

No religion is pure, and that is definitely the case with the religion of Christianity. So many people have been murdered, killed, and enslaved and brutally beaten, all in my name! That is a heavy load for me to carry, humanity. But even that is dissipating. I did not die for anyone's sins. I did not die (*chuckles*) on the cross!

You have been told repeatedly that any sins that you can conceive at this point are of your own doing. It is your soul's responsibility to teach, to teach you that there is no such thing as a sin—only poor judgment, poor choices for which you can forgive yourself.

The days ahead, Readers, may seem strange to you, for you will not be able to awake and think to yourself that this day will be like any other day. The days will change. You will no longer be able to count on a particular schedule, a particular way of reacting, of feeling, or being, or eating, or sleeping. Each day will be different. Turn your thoughts and energies over to the Father. Tell Him your concerns. Ask Him for the *forgiveness* (*energy*) to help you with letting go of many of your (*erroneous*) ideas.

God cannot make the changes for you. Only you can change your belief systems—only you. I AM Sananda and I tell you Readers to let go, let go and be flexible. Your age does not enter into this equation. If you are 80 years old, you can still be as a little child with joy and innocence waiting to see what is next for you. Do not be so hunkered down that you become afraid of change. We are with you; we are with you. I bless you all. I AM Sananda. (*Thank you, Lord.*)

Hello dear Readers, **I AM Lady Nada**. I am the Twin Flame, Twin Soul of Sananda. I am the higher soul of Mary Magdalene. It is always a joy to come forth and to say a few words. Many times I have spoken a few words in our books. Each time it may be a little repetitious, but it is done for a purpose, for the lessons build upon each other—the energies build.

We come to serve you. No issue or no matter is too small for us to help you with. Do not think that your problem is such a little problem to us that you cannot ask for help with it. As you know, little problems can grow into big problems and then you will find out that you ought to have asked for help a long time beforehand. So call upon us. We will be only too happy to bring you help.

Now you may not realize that you are receiving help, for there are angels that immediately go into action, but you will find that you will start to have clarity on a particular subject. You will start an action that will bring resolution to the supposed problem. All problems have solutions. It is your choice of your solution that makes the problem disappear or makes it multiply.

There is not much more that needs to be said for this chapter. Let us name this *Reflections of a Few*. Keep an open mind, Readers. As Sananda said, work on those belief systems, especially around religion. That is the one issue we see that will hold humanity back. Look how it is influencing the elections in America. Look at how the Fundamentalists think they are so right in their beliefs—in their most erroneous beliefs of Christianity. They feel they are so right that they even put labels of evil on that Brother of Light, Senator Barack Obama. Watch how you label people—how you label others. It has often been said that when you point one finger at someone, the other three are pointing back at you. If you do not quite get it, raise your hand and point and see the position of the other three of your fingers still curled and pointing toward you. Be careful with your labels. This is the political time in history where the labels can do much damage.

That is all I wish to say. I thank you for your time and I greet you with my love. I AM Lady Nada. (*Thank you, Lady.*) You are most welcome.

All right dear one, we have quite a potent little chapter here on Reflections... We shall call it quits for today. (Yes, thank you, Yeshua.)

*(Author's note: the Lord Kuthumi was Moses.)

CHAPTER 16- GODDESS QUAN YIN- COMPASSION of the HEART

Good morning everyone, we are back once again. One thing that you can count on is that we do not leave a project until it is finished. It does not matter how long a Channel needs to sit, how many days it will take, we do come and we give the information and we finish what we have started.

This Channel is more or less the same way. She takes on a project, in this case, her books, and before that her Dissertation for her Doctorate. She spends hours and hours thinking about what to say or what has been said. She thinks about it throughout the day. She has faith in what is being given to her (books).

Just this morning she had checked with her publishing company, Trafford, to view how her books were selling. It was not the money that she was interested in but where the books are being bought. She was delighted to see how many books had fanned out throughout the UK and even a few in Germany. What a delight to think that our words are fanning out over the world—what a delight.

If just one of you Readers was to pass on your book and then that person would pass on a book, the information would fan out even more. Not everyone has to buy a book for that is not the purpose. The purpose is in getting the information out. We are very gratified and it is a joy for us also.

Now this morning we have a Being coming who has been before but who wishes to speak again. Therefore, with the greatest delight we will let her step forward. I will come back at the end of her transmission.

Hello precious Readers, **I AM Goddess Quan Yin.**

GODDESS QUAN YIN- COMPASSION of the HEART

(*Oh, Quan Yin, how lovely to have you back!*) Thank you, dear soul, it is good to be back. Every once in a while I do like to come forward and stress the point of one's *caring, compassion, and mercy.* If you experience that energy, then you are carrying it! It is gratifying to me so see this energy of love, compassion, and mercy bloom in people. It is especially gratifying to see it bloom among the male population for so many times   they are caught up in their external world, and they equate compassion with sympathy. They may feel sympathy for someone and not realize they are judging that soul's experience, or that soul's learning process.

Those of you who are Readers of these books know by now that you set up these contracts before you are born. You set them up in order to learn different lessons that will in turn enhance those aspects of you. Many of you are honing different attributes and many of you are honing your attributes of compassion, mercy, love, and forgiveness—all part of the same energy.

Thereby, I reiterate to be aware that it is **compassion** that you wish to feel and not sympathy. When you feel compassion there is no judgment; there is heartfelt emotion coming from the heart with no blame, shame, or guilt—those devious *triplets,* as I call them. Therefore, I wish to name this chapter *Compassion of the Heart.*

I believe that most of you do not realize how many lifetimes you have had to have in order to learn compassion. It sounds simple enough, does it not? But it is one of the most difficult emotions to learn correctly—compassion, empathy, mercy and forgiveness are all part of the same energy.

When you see those fine men who have returned from war and have been maimed by explosions, burns and have lost limbs, how many of you go into sympathy and judgment—feeling your own energies, your own emotions, perhaps that range from frightening, even to a disgusting, abhorrence type of emotion?

GODDESS QUAN YIN- COMPASSION of the HEART

Many of those service men have chosen those experiences, as hard as it may be to believe that their souls would put them through this, but they chose those experiences in order to learn compassion. They have the most compelling stories of how one has given his life so that another may live. There is a camaraderie built around them. It becomes a club, does it not? They gather with each other and they cry and/or become angry and they curse and lose their faith, or they turn to faith for the first time. It is the human struggle that each one of them has to go through.

Each person, each service person who has been wounded, goes through his personal hell. He goes through his memory book of what it was like before he was burned beyond recognition; or what was it like before he lost his right hand; or what was it like before he lost his left leg? Many of them have even sadder stories where their loved one cannot cope with the partner's range of emotions and (*injuries*) and the loved one walks away, which adds even more pain. How many of those are broken contracts? Only the Karmic Board knows. How many of those have learned and have not evolved from those experiences? If any soul takes on a lifetime and says, *I need to hone my experience of compassion*, it is asking for a most difficult lesson indeed. It will entail a great sacrifice on their part, a great opportunity to become unselfish, and to help their fellow soldiers. The lessons are most remarkable.

Now here I am known as the Goddess of Mercy and Compassion. Have you thought of how I had to learn all of that? You are not just born and have it (*compassion*) bestowed upon you. These are learning experiences. And I had to learn this over thousands of years and hundreds of lifetimes. I told you in the previous book (*Your Space Brothers and Sisters Greet You! Chapter 6*) how I wanted to experience what it was like to come into a tiny, Chinese girl's body and have my feet bound. That was a learning experience—a very painful one.

GODDESS QUAN YIN- COMPASSION of the HEART

Now since the masculine and feminine energies must be balanced in my body, I chose lifetimes as a man in order to experience ways of learning compassion. Most ways of learning compassion are learned through wars, are they not—through skirmishes and attacks on another person? One is given opportunities to be brave and courageous. When you have a fellow soldier whose limb was cut off by the enemy, simply because he was protecting one of the men, you go through the whole gambit of emotions. You were told that if a certain man did not come forth and you did not divulge his name, you would lose a finger or a hand. You then had many choices to make, did you not? To hone compassion and mercy for a man always involved violence and wars and gangs. Even in ancient times there would be what you would call *gangs,* groups of like mind.

I took female lives in order to learn compassion. It usually generated around giving birth to stillborn babies, or having children die from disease, or being raped, or having a sibling raped. All of these acts of violence honed my compassion. By now one might ask *did you have any beautiful lives, Quan Yin, when you were learning all of this?* I would say there may have been fleeting moments, but since the lifetime was made for the purpose of learning compassion and having to come up with mercy of some kind, the situations were mostly dark.

Now this chapter might shock many of you Readers, but what it also is doing is bringing in reality. People are apt to think that the Goddesses and Masters are just Light and love without any of the human trials and tribulations. We have ascended; we have ascended from human life and that is what it means. When you ascend you have had these (*dark*) experiences.

Many of you who are reading these books have taken on lives that had very difficult lessons. You took on the life in order to experience what it is like to be what is called a *burn victim*, but as you know there is no such thing as a victim, for each has asked for that experience. I think that is one of the most difficult concepts for humanity—to realize that every horrible thing that they see and read about is a chosen lesson from the soul(s) involved. In that way, dear ones, you can bless that person for the courage it has taken to either learn that lesson or to hone that attribute. And yes, lessons can get out of hand. They can turn darker than was previously contracted for. However, there will be a balance; a balance will happen in order to transmute that energy.

One of the more difficult scenarios is when the soul returns Home and has its life review and realizes that it did not play the game correctly. It did not inch up the evolutionary ladder and hone its mercy and compassion. Therefore, it must experience another lesson that would bring that forth.

Not all of this is accomplished through violence. If the consciousness is such, one can have a lifetime of being a charity worker, such as Saint Mother Theresa. She gave her life to help those who were less fortunate than she. You can spend your lifetime helping, feeding, and caring for those who are less fortunate than you. In that way, you would learn compassion, if your lifetime were that selfless. You can die with all of your limbs and may have had a life where you owned little in the way of possessions, but you gained much in spiritual growth.

Compassion, Readers, sounds so flowery and yet when you know someone who has earned the title of being a compassionate soul, know that that soul has gone through his or her private hell. Know that that soul had asked for that experience.

That is all I wish to say, but I wanted to let you know that as the Earth goes more into her changes, as the dark fights harder and living becomes more difficult, that you all have chosen this time in history. Not only did you want to help in the transition, but you knew it would provide you an unprecedented opportunity to bring out the best in you—to

GODDESS QUAN YIN- COMPASSION of the HEART

bring out your compassion, caring, and loving heart. Every attribute has been earned repeatedly.

Therefore, when you hear of Quan Yin being the Goddess of Mercy and Compassion, know that she too had to learn that. She too has been where you may be at this moment. And she too now knows how your heart aches, how you feel, how you have sleepless nights, or how you have dreams of torment. I know this; I know what you are going through.

I give you my love; I give you my love. I AM the Goddess Quan Yin. Greetings. (*Thank you, Goddess.*) You are welcome, dear one, you are welcome.

All right, dear one, that was our precious Sister of Light bringing a sober lesson to people but one they need to hear, for so many of them think of us as just being in this love and Light without having had any of our own lessons and struggles. We are no different than you. We simply have just done it earlier than you and we are still climbing. Some day all of you will be saying to your students, "we are no different."

Greetings (tape runs out). 7-12-08

CHAPTER 17- ASHTAR INVITES YOU ONCE AGAIN

Yeshua: Good morning, precious one, you received some e-mails this morning that were disturbing to you. (Yes) Dearest one, let us talk about "judgments" for a minute or two. When people who you know and love do not understand where you are coming from and they go into judgment about what it is you are doing, can you allow them to be where they are? Can you allow them to form their opinion, whether it agrees with yours or not?

That is where they are in their consciousness. They know no different. It is the growth of the soul that will change that. They will change someday, but for now that is the way it is. Also many people have merged with their partners and therefore, their energies are mixed. One partner may not be as conscious as the other, which keeps everyone more or less at a status quo. Judgments, dear one... Everyone has and makes judgments. They do not realize what they are doing or the danger of doing it.

You also received e-mails that were defaming Senator Barack Obama. People do not understand where he is coming from. They see him as a "change-coat," flip-flopping from one position to another, letting the public down. They do not understand the game that he is playing, the tightrope that he is walking. He is on his path to becoming president, but there are so many pit-falls along the way. He struggles at times and is surprised also at some of the attacks that he receives. And yet there is something in him that keeps him going forward— the perseverance. If all goes as is planned, he will become president. Then the changes that he has promised the people during the primaries will be implemented. He is well aware of the different roles he is playing, but always with one goal in mind—to become president.

ASHTAR INVITES YOU ONCE AGAIN

He is not doing this from ego. He is being driven by an inner force of Light—an inner purpose that he knows is his destiny. It is similar to people in sports. For example, the famous ice skaters were on skates almost before they could walk. They had that desire to perform those awesome jumps. The equestrian riders are the same—always the love of their horses is the focus of their lives.

Therefore, Readers, it is not fitting for you to judge others either in their professions or in their everyday lives, for each is doing his or her purpose. This Author writes books. It is her purpose at this time. You have followed her writings from the beginning. You have watched her develop into an author. You have watched her become stronger in her transmissions. You have watched as her books have fanned out into different countries.

Some people may ask, "What is the purpose of this?" I can reply, "What is the purpose of anything?" There is always a purpose that remains in the hands of that person's soul. That person's soul has the purpose. Judgments of another's purpose become difficult when that person recognizes that he or she is being judged. It hurts; it is painful. In some instances it can stop people from continuing their purpose. Parents must always be cognizant of this, for so many times they want their children to follow in their footsteps. Maybe that is not the direction that the child was supposed to take. Just know, Readers, when you sit opposite people in your family, or when you pass people on the street, that that soul has a purpose for doing what he or she is doing. That person must not be judged by family or humanity. There is that saying "judge not, for what you judge, you will become." It is not quite that simple but it is close enough.

We prefer the term "to allow." Allow that person to be who he or she is. If you allow that then you are not judging, for in judging there are hidden messages: "I do not like what you are doing; do it my way. It does not sound that productive to me; do it my way."

ASHTAR INVITES YOU ONCE AGAIN

Now we will continue our book this morning and the next Presenter is standing by.

Good morning everyone, **I AM Ashtar**. (*Oh, Ashtar, hello!*) Hello, dear soul, I do love coming in and speaking with you (*Readers*). In our last book (*Your Space Brothers and Sisters Greet You!*) we spoke quite often of our spaceships. Therefore, we thought it only appropriate to have a chapter about the ships since this book is about the teachings of the various Masters.

As most of you know I, Commander Ashtar, am of the Federation of Light of the Galactic Command. There is still much of humanity that does not believe in spaceships. They would rather believe their government when it says that it is a hoax; those are weather balloons; nothing ever happened in New Mexico; there was never a crashed spacecraft; there were never dead bodies of aliens found. Your government has so many reasons why it will not give the truth to humanity. I will say that all of that was true! There will be no more secrets in that closet. Some people are coming to the realization of that. We have to commend Larry King, for he keeps trying, letting his listeners know about UFOs. (*Larry King Live, TV 7-18-08.*)

This Channel lives in the Phoenix area of Arizona. While she did not see those famous *Phoenix Lights* in the sky, that truly happened. Those were our ships. You will see many more sightings of the ships, for that is your future. We are showing you a glimpse of your future.

As you look to the sky and see airplanes fly over, you pay little attention to them. Or, you may exclaim, *look at that plane; look at the chem trails.* This Channel lives near Luke Air Force Base and frequently its planes are flying over the house in their practice maneuvers. She watches them with amazement on how closely they fly.

Picture this, Readers. You may not hear a sound, but if

151

ASHTAR INVITES YOU ONCE AGAIN

you look up, you may see spaceships in the sky. This is going to happen, so you might as well start getting used to it. You will see these spaceships. We will put on a little show just so you will know who we are. We can be stationary and then zoom off in a blink of an eye. We can reappear instantly, if we decide to uncloak our machine, making it visible once again. We do this for your benefit. We do this so you will start getting used to us and not be afraid. We will come in greater number just to show you there is nothing to fear.

With the work of our many Lightworkers, who we fondly refer to as our *ground crew*, the public is becoming informed of our nearness, our coming to you, and our intention. Our intention is not to harm you in any way. That is truly of the past and science fiction. When the less-conscious ships came in the past, they were searching for Earth's water, minerals, crystals, and gold. They did not care so much about the humans, but they were curious, so they would bring them aboard and study them—every inch of them and many times in painful ways.

Therefore, when you have all of that as a precursor to our coming—our ships of Light, consciousness, and spirituality—all of that previous dark energy influences the way you would think of us now. If you as children were read tales of gross evil gnomes and elves doing evil things flying around in evil ships, you were programmed. As an adult you will remember that past programming so that it becomes difficult to change your way of thinking to the idea that maybe our ships are of Light. Just maybe these ships will have something positive to teach us.

However, Readers, it does depend on your consciousness, does it not? If you are at the level of such physicality that you cannot think outside of your box, it would be most difficult and scary for you to see a space ship hovering over your city, land, or your house. And yet those of higher consciousness know that those are ships of Light and love.

ASHTAR INVITES YOU ONCE AGAIN

Look at all of the bad press that the crop circles have generated. Those crop circles were made by technology from starships. They are geometric messages. The designs are beautiful and so precise as seen from the air. They boggle the mind because of their intricate beauty. And yet they carry profound messages that are not always interpreted correctly. However, are those not precursors to the fact that there are ships from other planets? The disbelievers attempt to replicate those crop circles. Some have been able to in a crude way, making a simple design. However, the intricate designs are impossible for human machinery to make. It is impossible.

When Yeshua started this chapter, he was saying to allow people their judgments, for you cannot change anyone but yourself, as I am sure you have heard for eons of time. Therefore, how can one justify these beautiful crop circles? It is only by allowing the fact that space visitors have come and left a calling card. This is their calling card; this is their business card. *We will not harm you. We are giving you messages from space. Allow us to be what we are—ships of Light, love, and spirituality.*

In our previous book, we talked much about the fact that you would be given a choice to come aboard, to visit our ships for a short duration. We are not saying we will zoom you up forever. We are merely saying we offer you that hotel in the sky. People go on vacations and they have planned where they will have a wonderful meal and spend the night. They have a motel or a hotel picked out as to where they will stay.

Well, that is what we are offering you, a journey, and a vacation to that fabulous resort in the sky. You will learn so much, for what you will be doing is stepping into the future. You may not know it but what we will be showing you **is** your future. This is what it will be like when people are reincarnated years from now. You will step into the future and experience a way of living that is not even in your imagination. If you think about it, look at the assortment of the beautiful flowers that you have on Earth. There are the exquisite roses, lilies, so many varieties of flowers, and pansies with their little faces with petals so soft you might want to hold them next to your cheek. However, do you think that those flowers were always on Earth? NO, various Masters brought them here. The rose is attributed to Mother Mary. That is her flower.

And yet if you had come to Earth, which many of you had, before any of those flowers were here, you would not be able to describe them. You would not be able to describe that gorgeous lily, the whiteness of it and the way it curves like a chalice with a beautiful orange stamen in the center of it—the glorious lily. But you would not be able to describe it nor paint it for it was in your future. Then you died and came back and saw lilies and roses.

It will be similar with Mother Earth after her various changes and people have lived out their lifespan according to their contracts. They then come back years hence and may find that some of the things that they saw on the ships are now commonplace on Earth. Your transportation could be built on air.

Twenty five years or so ago, this Channel had a dream that the train that commuted through the underground tunnel, known as the *tube*, between Oakland, California, and San Francisco Bay, was traveling silently at a tremendous speed. It rode on a cushion of air. She knew that she was looking at train travel of the future. Therefore, we say to come aboard our ships. It is your choice. Come aboard our ships and live your future! Won't that be exciting, to live your future? Then at the end of your life cycle and you again come back to Earth, you will remember, for the memory will be in your cells. *I know what this is like. I must have lived in the future.*

I AM Ashtar of the Galactic Command saying to you, *be not afraid of our ships, for we will come and we will come in mass to help you, to offer our services and to give you a choice of spending some time with us in that hotel in the sky. I hope we will see you there.*

I give you my blessings, greetings.

(Thank you Ashtar, how do you want to name this chapter?) You could just say *Ashtar Invites You Once Again. (OK)*

Yeshua: that's it for today, dear one, see you in a couple of days. Greetings.

CHAPTER 18- SANAT KUMARA'S WORDS

*Hello everyone, the gang's all here once again to bring in another chapter. Actually, I ought to have said to **help** bring in another chapter for it is this Channel who does all the work. We merely stand by, introducing the different Beings of Light and taking great pleasure in our task—great pleasure.*

This morning we are bringing forth another great Being that has spoken before in the previous books but has yet to make himself known in this one. Therefore, I will step aside now and let him come forth.

Good morning everyone, **I AM** known to the world as **Sanat Kumara**. *(Oh, Lord, it has been so long since I last talked with you!)* And yet in our world it only seems to have been a short while. Since this book is about the Teachings of the different Masters of Light, let me bring forth a teaching that is dear to my heart.

You have been taught about love, the giving and the receiving; you have been taught about the different aspects of compassion and mercy; you have been taught about allowing and you have been taught about releasing belief systems— and yet all of those teachings have a common thread, do they not?

That common thread, dear souls, is the love one needs to have for one's neighbors—the love one needs to have for humanity. So much of the world is going through a difficult time at this point as the Earth shakes off the darker energies and brings about the changes that she envisions. How many times have you been told or it has been suggested to share what you have with those who have less?

There is a great energy coming upon the planet that many of you have been cognizant of and it is being called the 8-

SANAT KUMARA'S WORDS

8-8, which is actually August, the 8th month, and the 8th day in the year of 2008. This energy is one of Abundance, which is also the abundance of one's attributes. What attributes do you have? Is a generous heart one of your attributes—being willing to share what little you may have, or to share what abundance that you may have? It is a great joy to watch people share from the heart. That is all part of loving thy neighbor. Your neighbor does good deeds for you and you share, giving back but perhaps not in kind, perhaps not monetarily, but in other ways.

This is all sharing; this is all part of honoring your neighbor. Do unto others... That is one of the greatest teachings that the Lord Jesus/Yeshua/Sananda brought onto the planet. And yet today people seem to forget that, for if a neighbor has something that they covet, they try in a greedy way to obtain it. This can be done through theft, hold-ups, robberies, and/or wars with other countries.

Every time you turn on the television news, you see reports where another bank has been held up, where a neighbor has been robbed—people coveting someone else' abundance. The world is going through its own metamorphosis. It is changing its skin. It is no longer allowing people to take— to take of the Earth's resources, taking its oil, taking its minerals, taking its crystals, its diamonds, its gold, its silver, its coal—always taking. Where is love thy neighbor? Where is love thy Earth—thy Mother Gaia?

I am known as the *Lord of the World,* and your world is in dire straits at this time. Is it not reasonable that someday all of the evil—the taking energies, the greed, the lack of sharing—is it not reasonable that some day that all will be transmuted? The polarization of this planet will be greatly lessened. It will take many years, centuries before the polarization will have dissipated.

However, when Heaven merges with Earth, then you will know. People with their dark hearts will be sent to other spheres so that eventually everyone on the planet will be of similar heart. There will still be differences, for personalities may clash, but the heart energy will be similar. If anyone is in trouble, the heart energies will supersede any of the personality/ego problems.

The world will be changing at a faster rate than you will be able to imagine. Most of you really have no idea. The young people coming to the planet now truly are the future of the planet. They will be helping with the Abundance energy, for they will live it, you see. It will be in their mentality. They come in knowing there is no lack in God's World, in the Universe. There is no lack. There are only man-made restrictions superimposed on the public.

The banking situation is starting to fail, as you have noticed, for its foundation is not built upon gold or silver assets but built upon paper. Many banks will fail and close their doors but then reopen in a healthier and more productive way. The teachings I am giving you this morning are varied. They cover many subjects: the sharing, doing unto others, caring for your neighbors, caring for the Earth, allowing and knowing that God of this Universe is watching, that God of this planet is in your heart waiting for you to make conscious contact, waiting for His guidance. If each person in this world would listen to his or her heart—the God of his heart, the I AM Presence—lack, greed, coveting would all disappear.

People must change their mentality. There is a shift—a paradigm shift—that needs to happen. That shift needs to be that you **know** that there is no lack, that you will always have what you need. The shift is to realize that what you **think** you need is far more—exorbitantly so—than what you really need. In other words, is there moderation with your wants and needs? There **is** abundance, but there also needs to be balance and moderation.

Not everyone needs to have millions in the bank and live in 7,000 square foot houses. NO, that's the point. It is

SANAT KUMARA'S WORDS

the paradigm shift here. You need to live in moderation and balance. You can have one or two cars, but you do not need ten! You can have a few pieces of beautiful jewelry, but you do not need dozens of rings, bracelets, and necklaces, for that can become greed; that is possession. You do not truly **need** that.

The paradigm shift then is from what you **think** you need or want to what you **really** need. If people could only be happy within a very generous way of living without excesses, knowing they could always have it if they want it... How many times have you heard about someone who has won the lottery and two or three years later the person is broke again because of excessive spending on cars, jewelry, houses, and yachts? It gets to the point where there is no longer anything that you can buy that you really want. You give it away and you give it away. Now if you had started and had just shared in moderation with those who needed help, knowing that you could buy anything that you want...

Change the belief system; make that paradigm shift. It is living generously but still in moderation because you know it will always be there for you. This is what humanity needs—to know the abundance is always there. Now will this happen overnight? Of course not, as long as you have nations of people who are starving, the genocides, all the evil that is going on because people think they are in lack. That mentality has to shift. That is where the paradigm shift needs to happen. And it will, but perhaps not as quickly as you would like it to. Nothing changes overnight—certainly not humanity's belief systems.

Therefore, Readers, look at what you have. Look at how you are behaving in the world, how you give to your neighbors, how you walk in Light with a pure heart, how your thoughts are clear, and whether you know you have abundance in all areas of your life—emotionally, spiritually, and physically. The energy is coming in in huge waves. You can call it waves of consciousness, waves of energy. The waves will change humanity. If people cannot change and their contracts are up and they pass on to the other side, they will be removed from Earth. Those of the darker minds who wage greedy wars will be removed.

I leave you this day with this message: to open your hearts, take a thorough inventory of your bodies—physical, mental, emotional, spiritual bodies—and see if you have any energy of lack or poverty consciousness in your bodies. Work with your energies. Do not take them for granted. Transmute energies that need to change. Open your hearts to full abundance, full consciousness, and full love of your neighbors.

I AM Sanat Kumara.

(Thank you, Lord, and for those who need a bit more introduction of who you are, will you please say what your role is in the world right now?)

I AM the World Teacher, but I spend a great deal of my time on Venus. I will be turning over my baton to someone else, for my work is done on this planet. But since I am still attached somewhat, I come and speak with different people. Therefore, let us call this chapter Sanat Kumara's Words.

(Thank you, Lord.) You are welcome.

All right, dear one, that does it for today. We still have a few more chapters, and then it will be time to wrap the book up. We will be back in a few days. Greetings.

CHAPTER 19- MOTHER MARY COMMENTS

Good morning, precious one, and to all of our Readers, we are back once again to proceed with this book that is progressing very nicely but will shortly be coming to an end. I know, it is always difficult to realize that there will be an end to something that you are enjoying. For you Readers who always want the next book and the next book and the next book, there must always be an ending, must there not? Therefore, we will be bringing an ending to this book one of these days, but not yet, dear souls, not yet.

Today we have a Presenter for you, a woman. We always need to keep that energy balanced in our books as we have taught you. This woman has spoken before and she is greatly loved. So I will step aside now and let her come forth, for she always has teachings of great worth, and this book is about the Teachings of the Masters of Light. I now step aside.

Good morning my children and my blessed Readers, good morning to all, **I AM** known as your **Mother Mary**, but some just call me **Mother** while some call me the **Divine Mother**, whatever. (*Chuckles*) I am not that tied up in my names. I wonder how many of you are? So many times when people get married they turn their identity over to their husbands, especially if they marry a military man of high rank, or if they marry a professional man like a doctor, shall we say. They become the Colonel's wife, or they become the doctor's wife. They lose their identity.

Some people, however, are becoming more cognizant of this fact so that they are keeping their own name on that marriage certificate. We think that is a *good thing*, to use your saying. It is a good thing for you do need to keep your own identities. In the theatrical world, men who are married

MOTHER MARY COMMENTS

to famous women tend to be known as so and so's husband, whereby they lose their identity. Then that wounds the male ego, since with male energy, his world is the external world. If he no longer has his own identity, he becomes angry and at times vicious so that he may strike out to the point of striking his beloved wife.

Humanity, as you go through your difficult stages in order to advance in your own evolutions, you have heard how the shadow parts of you will come forward in order for you to acknowledge that they are part of you. *Yes, I am judgmental at times; yes, I do envy people at times; yes, I can be an angry person as I look back at the abuse I took during my childhood; yes, I can be selfish and greedy and egotistical.* But, dear hearts, now that you have admitted you have those shadow parts of yourself, you have a choice: *I choose not to come from greed; I choose to be less egotistical; I choose to be less judgmental; I choose the Light versus my dark side; I choose to watch my thoughts; I choose to love my neighbor.* That last statement is one of the most difficult ones to embrace, is it not?

The Lord Sanat Kumara was speaking about loving thy neighbor. You see, when you love thy neighbor, you must bring in your forgiveness energies. You must come from the heart because there are areas within yourself that you need to forgive. In that way you can forgive what you perceive is going on with your neighbor.

Now when we use the term *neighbor*, we are not speaking specifically about the person next door but those who are sitting around you in a restaurant, or those you are sitting with you on a bus, or those that you are sitting with in a schoolroom. These are all neighbors. The different counties where you live are neighbors; the different areas to which you travel are neighbors.

And yes, some of your neighbors are more desirable to know than others. My blessed Son, Yeshua, whom you called

MOTHER MARY COMMENTS

Jesus, was able to view his neighbors—the people who crowded around him and tore at his garments, taking and taking, wanting *a piece* of him, as you say—he was able to see that those were truly his neighbors. Were they not souls? Were they not children of God? Of course they were.

He saw the frailties of the body. He saw the frailties of the mind and the frailties of the emotions. He saw their veils, hiding the magnificent souls that they were. He saw this! His heart then expanded even further. His love expanded further until it was like a blanket that would come over the crowd, a blanket of love, peace, and forgiveness. They would leave feeling that they had been touched by God.

This is how he earned his reputation of being God. Now, you have been told in previous books that one of the higher parts of Yeshua is Sananda, and indeed Sananda and Christ Michael, the One you call God, were in that body. Therefore, they **were** being touched by God. However, the people were not able to make that differentiation. Remember they were only third dimensional people and some were even second dimensional people, still just barely on the path. Or we shall put it another way since they had not discovered a path to be on—they were barely awakening in consciousness.

And yet this man, who you know as Yeshua, could see them as they truly were—beautiful souls who had taken bodies in order to experience the history-making events that surrounded the man, Jesus. Many of you today were back in that generation. Many of you today, therefore, are having a most difficult time, you see, in being able to discern what is truth now.

Where has religion gone wrong? Where has Christianity become bent? Well, you have also received the information that all religions did not start from a truthful base, for the scribes, priests, and rabbis took the words of the prophets and turned them into religion. The dark forces whom you call the *Illuminati* started these religions, as you have been told.

Therefore, here you are in the 21st century, back from having lived in those Biblical times. You are now questioning those religions; you are questioning what you had been taught all through your developing years. You are asking, *Did my Lord really heal people? Was my Lord really crucified? Did my Lord really die on the Cross?* Some people do not think of Yeshua as being their Lord, which is really correct. He **is no one's Lord**, for that would be possessing him, would it not? He is a Master Teacher, a Teacher of the greatest Light that there will ever be on this Earth. And yet he has been maligned so dreadfully by humanity.

As we have said, one of the worst times was when the Catholic priests tried to convert humanity to their way of thinking. They would send out missionaries to save the "savages" in the tropical lands. Throughout South America, throughout Mexico, the Spaniards went carrying their distorted words, wearing outrageous clothes, for any sight of the flesh was supposedly an abomination to God.

How ridiculous, for God made your body. How would He think it is abominable to wear a bathing suit? Can you picture these sanctimonious bearers of distorted truth coming onto islands—where the humidity and the heat would want anyone in his or her right mind to take off some clothes—and then to force the natives to cover their flesh? Also remember there was no such thing as air conditioning or deodorants. It merely added to the stench, did it not? Humanity is so silly at times.

As you look back throughout history, you can read about the many mistakes that have been made all in the name of creating Saints or gurus or whatever they could find to worship, not knowing the only guru ought to be God. Have you ever thought of God as being your personal Guru? He

MOTHER MARY COMMENTS

is getting a chuckle out of this, for He has a fine sense of humor. That is the Guru you ought to be worshipping.

I come today not only because I enjoy speaking with you, communing with you, but I also come in seriousness, for it is an opportunity for me to reiterate or to stress various teachings for different areas of your life. The United States, of course, is all wrapped up in the elections and the different candidates. Your Senator Barack Obama is walking a fine line indeed, for he was being criticized for not having gone to Europe and visiting the different countries. Now he is being criticized for having done so and therefore, his trip is all a *political ruse*.

That is where the saying comes in, *You're damned if you do and you're damned if you don't.* And YES, I, Mother Mary, can say that once in a while (*chuckling*), for we do not think of it as being a curse. It is just a silly word, but it does bring to your attention how nasty politics can be. It can be finger pointing. It can destroy people. If enough negativity is sent to a person, it can stop that person from fulfilling his purpose.

Now is Senator Obama always correct in what he says? Not necessarily, nor is his opponent, Senator John McCain, who is a courageous soldier of the past. But you see, Readers, that is one of the problems for America, is it not? Senator McCain is in that generation of the past. It is very difficult for people to see his being able to move beyond that.

Each generation brings a different energy. This Channel is a senior, and she works hard at keeping abreast of what is going on. However, she has found that the age of computers and electronics has gotten beyond her. She does not understand iPODS and Blackberries. She has no desire to download iTunes, but you see that becomes then a generational gap. Therefore, what we are saying is that that does not necessarily make her wrong; it just means that *time marches forward!* It just means that people in Senator

MOTHER MARY COMMENTS

McCain's generational era are most likely out of touch. They do not know how to change. Many of them do not want to change.

Thereby, here comes Senator Obama who is from a different generation—with a very intelligent, brilliant mind—and he is all for change, of course, for that is his generation. You can bet he knows computers and cell phone systems. That is his generation. Therefore, America has choices here. It is difficult to keep up with the changes when you are a senior. Many seniors do not own computers and consequently do not know how to traverse the Internet and nor how to e-mail people.

Readers, all people need to strive to keep changing, to keep afresh with new ideas, to keep going forward, for if they do not, they will stagnate and then their soul realizes that its time of gaining wisdom from learning is coming to a close. Therefore, it is time to go Home.

Always be ready and willing to change. One of the things we have noticed is people's thoughts, their belief systems; they will not change those beliefs, not realizing that they are bringing stagnation to their body. One must keep going forward; keep going forward!

This Channel put off buying a new computer a year ago for she knew it would be a difficult task learning a new system. She was worried about all the files she had for her books that were stored in her old computer *(and would have to be transferred to a new computer.)* However, it was on her birthday on August 24th of last year that she gave herself what she calls her *birthday gift* of a new computer system. She bought an HP laptop that she dearly loves. Converting to the new way of learning that system has not been easy for her, but she has persevered.

Therefore, you see that one must be willing to change. One must be willing to go forward. It is your thought processes

MOTHER MARY COMMENTS

that stop you. *Oh, learning about all that stuff is too much trouble.* That stops your growth and you do not realize that you are bringing stagnation to your body. Now, you may be advancing in other areas and that is commendable, for you then are going forward and making changes there. Always be open to change.

Change is inevitable. Everything is going to change after the election. Know that, but be willing to embrace what those changes are; be willing to proceed in the direction that history is marching toward. That history, of course, is 2012, which is not the cut-off date where the world is to end. It is merely closing the door on one consciousness and opening up to a new consciousness of the Golden Age. It is ending cycle with your way of acting and your old way of thinking.

The old ways... Be willing to let them go; be willing to embrace what is being offered to you, to leave the poverty consciousness and to embrace the abundance consciousness—the abundance that you know God has stored for you in Heaven that is absolutely bottomless. Your abundance is a free-flowing energy. It is you who stops the flow. If you think that you cannot have something that you would really like but you were afraid because of the cost of it and then did not buy it, you stopped yourself. Do you not know that no matter what it is that you want in moderation is always affordable for you—anything you wish? A small amount of cherries for seven dollars sounds exorbitant but if you wish to have cherries in their short season, why do you not buy them?

Think of it this way: *Well, if the cherries were two dollars, I would be saving five dollars and then I would buy them. But then where would I spend that extra five dollars? On something else that perhaps I do not particularly need?* Always question, stop and think. Now you need to realize that there is a difference between seven dollars worth of cherries and seventy thousand dollars for a new car, for there

MOTHER MARY COMMENTS

would be no moderation in that. But give to yourself. Know that you can afford those seven dollars' worth of cherries.

Be willing to change your thought processes; be willing to change. That is my teaching for today, dear Readers. Thank you for the time that you will spend reading this chapter.

Until we meet again, I AM Mary.

(*Thank you Lady*.) You are welcome, dearest Channel, daughter of my heart; you are welcome.

CHAPTER 20- AA MICHAEL- YEARNINGS

Yeshua: Good morning and blessings to all of you, this is our twentieth chapter! We still have some Presenters to come forth, however. Much is going on in your world right now. There is a speeding up of the energies, as you know. That is somewhat of a dichotomy, because as the energies speed up, many bodies are experiencing being lethargic, having problems centering and grounding and being focused on their purposes.

However, rest assured, Readers, it is the energy; it is the energy. All of this will change and will balance out, for it is bringing you into a higher level of consciousness—a level that many of you perhaps have not experienced before. Fifth dimensional consciousness is love, you see, and some of you have a difficult time in receiving love and knowing what love is all about. However, you are learning; you are learning. I will step aside now for a great one wishes to speak.

Good morning to this delightful group of Readers. **I AM** known as the **Archangel Michael**. I have spoken to you before among these pages, and I do so now for I wish to bring to your attention some more teachings. Some of you may already know this; some of you may read this as new material. However, just know that all of you already have this information and know this information, for it is in your cells.

When you take a body and come upon the Earth, you bring with you memories of the past. You bring with you the formulations that you have made throughout history. Most of you Readers are millions of years old—what we would call *old souls*. It is the old souls that reach for a book such as ours, for they are searching; they are searching for that past memory. There is something missing in their lives. They do not know what it is. They may have private bouts of crying.

Some cry while in the shower. It is hidden, for then the water hides the tears and the noise of the flowing water hides the sound of their sobbing. When they come out of the shower, they may not understand what has taken place. They are puzzled by what they have just emitted. If they are men, they may be somewhat ashamed. If they are women, they are more apt to go inward and search as to *why am I crying? Is it my depression returning? Do I need more medication?*

We say to you it is you searching for that connection with you! You are seeking that higher I AM Presence of yourself. You are yearning to know your soul at the deepest level. You are yearning to be in the Presence of God once again. It is that **yearning**, dear ones, that causes you to sob. You are searching; you are searching for the higher parts of you.

Most of you know, although some may not, that you have various levels of higher parts of yourself. Just when you think you have become acquainted with one part of yourself, you advance again and find that indeed there is another aspect of yourself (*even your future-self*) that you did not know existed. It resides in the higher realms and is holding the focus for you. It is holding many of your past attributes. It is holding much of your past wisdom. You have come to a crossroads in this lifetime. Your higher souls have sent you down, if you wish to use that explicit phrase for it bears a picture, does it not? It bears a picture of you descending that ladder of evolution in order to glean the last bit of wisdom from this present earthly experience.

When you reach the end of your earthly days, the end of your contract, and pass over to Nirvana, many of you will go forward. You may go on to other planets and make other journeys, still searching for new ways to accomplish your tasks.

AA MICHAEL- YEARNINGS

You are not unlike Christopher Columbus (who was our great Saint Germain) who sailed away in his ships to discover new worlds. You have a purpose and that purpose is to seek wisdom; you (*continuously*) wish for more wisdom.

If you are over a million of years old, can you not visualize the amount of wisdom that you carry? It is written in the Books of Life and you have volumes of those Books. You have libraries just about you! Your wisdom and your Books could fill a library here on Earth—totally about you, for you have lived for millions of years. Is that not an awesome thought to know that you have your personal library and that you carry volumes, Encyclopedias of wisdom?

Then you take an Earth life as you have taken this last one. You journey down through all the layers, all the levels of selves of you. Each time you step further down it becomes denser. You then start to forget as you reach the bottom rung and your mother births you with a push of pain and many times with a scream, matching your scream as you come out into this world, a world you were not totally prepared for. YES, you had instruction; YES, you even viewed the world on different monitors and your guides, angels, teachers, and mentors discussed with you what you would see, what you would be up against. Then your soul, your I AM Presence, sent you forth with its blessings.

You had the first seven of your years learning to be your own person, *to stand on your own two feet*, as the saying goes. You are molded into the person that you will be by the age of seven. Now it all depends, of course, on how much your family, siblings, and teachers programmed you as to what the final mold was by the age of seven. It has been written that you accrue no karma within those first seven years, but some of that is changing because some of the young bodies are maturing faster and may have turned to dark energies before the age of seven.

Therefore, here you are an adult and you have married,

divorced, remarried, or divorced again or stayed single. You have had so many choices for what lay ahead of you. You made choices blindly and many times without any wisdom pertaining to them. Then you had to struggle with the psychological repercussions—the guilt, the anguish, the feeling of not feeling loved, the feeling of abandonment, perhaps, outrage and anger. If you were males, you became violent and slapped people around and struck out and became bullies, perhaps.

If you went further into your darker energies, you would buy guns and shoot people. Then you would spend time in prison and meet many people of like-minds. In there you would have many more choices, would you not? There is a group mind that forms in those prisons, and it would be up to you to break out of that. Some find God in those cells; some finish their education; some acquire college degrees. Many of those inmates were there because it was the soul's purpose to learn—to learn about the shadow world.

People who read these books, however, are from another layer of consciousness. They yearn for the spiritual world. They yearn for spirituality, knowing God, knowing about the vastness of the Heavenlies. Many of you embrace the fact that there are angels and Archangels and that we are truly real. Many of you see us in actuality but invariably you put wings on us. I will say we accept them (*chuckles*), but we ourselves do not create them out of necessity.

You have seen formal dress for men. You have the tuxedo and then even more formal are the tails. Well, angels can create wings if they wish to present themselves that way— at the top of their formal attire. However, wings are not necessary. We do not fly around with wings, but they can be very beautiful—very soft, pure white, and quite lovely.

So what have I brought this morning to teach you? **I came to emphasize the fact that what you are yearning for, what you are crying for, is your own soul!** How does

174

one recognize one's soul? Some do it through meditation. Some do it with just knowing. Some have techniques where they will deep breathe until they eventually recognize their own energy.

When this Channel was first developing her spirituality and during the time that she was giving her Doctoral Address upon receiving her Doctorate, she felt such a command of her words. She was articulate; she was humorous; she emanated joy and love. People came up to her afterwards and hugged her and told her how wonderful her speech was and did not know that what they had experienced had been soul energy.

She had been studying under a group of Teachers and they told her afterwards that they had helped bring her soul 85% into her body. Readers, 85% is a tremendous number, for most people are only in their bodies around 10%. Picture that; picture how you would feel if you had 85% of yourself in your body.

Afterwards, this Channel told friends that she felt as though she had had a *spiritual experience,* for she was in such bliss, such control of the moment. She gave her address without memorization, without notes, and she said that the information just flowed. **That** dear Readers is soul energy. **That** is what you are yearning for.

Now could she maintain the 85% of soul energy in her body? NO, as much as she would have liked to, she could not, for her body was being bombarded by the density of the environment in the world. When one is walking in such density, it is nigh impossible for the average person to have his soul in his body that much. It does not happen. And yet as she has advanced in years, she has studied and has done all the things that you most likely are doing—the workshops, seminars, body-energy work, and the pure thoughts—all the things that you have done and are still doing have brought her soul in closer and closer. Now is her soul-Light at 100%?

AA MICHAEL- YEARNINGS

NO, but she has managed to bring herself in at a very high percentage point indeed.

We will say that soul energy is a different energy than you expect to have. There is such clarity within you when your soul is fully present. The choices are more pure. The joy, the humor... It is quite amazing, people. So I say this is what you are searching for; this is what you miss, for you know there is something more. Many of you search outside of yourselves. That is why there are so many love affairs, marriages, and divorces. Not only are you ending cycle but you are also searching for one who will bring you total fulfillment, not realizing that you are searching for yourself.

When you have found yourself, you will have found peace, contentment, love, Light, joy, humor, and forgiveness. You will have all those attributes honed to a magnificent level. All those attributes that you attribute to the Masters will be yours, for you will have then finally merged with the Master that you are—with your higher selves. Keep searching, but be very clear in your minds that what you are seeking, trying to find, is not outside of yourself and certainly not in another person. **It is yourself that you are seeking. It is You** with a capital **Y**.

I AM Archangel Michael and I serve you this day.

CHAPTER 21- MARY MAGDALENE'S LITTLE STORY

Good morning everyone, it is I, Yeshua, back once again to continue our book. It has come to our observation that those who search for meaning in their lives are apt to come to books such as these. They are looking for something beyond the dogma of their religious teachings. They know when they come upon a book such as ours that they have found it. It gives them such joy. Most of them read the book more than once, basking in the energies, not wanting to put it down.

That ties in actually with what Archangel Michael was saying in the previous chapter. Our books trigger that yearning in you—the yearning for your soul, that higher self. That is one of its purposes among many. We have given you another piece to your puzzle, another key to your awakening.

This morning we are bringing back a woman Presenter whom we have had before. There is still much to say. This is a good spot among these pages to bring forth her message. I step aside now so that my beloved may speak.

Hello once again everyone, **I AM Mary Magdalene** and I blend with my higher self, **Lady Nada**, for we are one. This Channel has a CD playing an old hymn in the background, *How Great Thou Art*. Now we understand that many of those old hymns may not be politically correct, may sound too religious, may contain dogmatic statements, may not be totally true, but always check to see if you resonate with the energy of the music, for that is what these old hymns are. They are energetic reminders of your higher selves, your soul, and of your God. As I listen to the words, they are moving indeed. They can bring tears to your eyes if you really embrace the words—*How Great Thou Art; How Great Thou Art. (A long pause ensues as she listens to the music.)*

MARY MAGDALENE'S LITTLE STORY

This morning, dear Readers, I wish to tell you a little story, for many times it is an easy way of conveying a particular teaching and making a point.

Once in one of my lifetimes I was a little girl. I chose a lifetime where I would not be the center of attraction—where I would not be that loved. I was not the beauty in the family and no one thought that I would marry. So I willingly put myself in the background and let my sister shine. She was the beauty. She was the star attraction wherever she went. She had many beaus flirting with her, wanting to court her. She played them for all they were worth.

In those days (with people of the higher classes), the morals among the young females were very strict. The young girls did not give themselves sexually to their suitors until their wedding night. Nor would their suitors want them to. Many times they tried, for their hormones were running rampant, as the saying goes. They would have been sorely disappointed if they had won their little passionate game. Therefore, while my sister had many suitors, she waited as the pure girl that she was until she had made her choice.

For me, I just did what my mother told me to do. I did housework, I studied; I played outside. Then I was at the Essene Community (*in Mt. Carmel*), for my family thought it would bring spiritual teachings to me that could provide advancement for me. I was so unhappy. I tried everything that I could think of in ways of manipulation to keep from having to do my *duties* and what I thought were menial jobs.

As young children will, I thought I was being punished and that was why they were so strict with me. I even went on a hunger strike. I tried everything to keep from learning. It was during that time that I was befriended by a young girl who also was unhappy, for her mother had died and her father had gone off and joined another community leaving her in the hands of the Essenes.

MARY MAGDALENE'S LITTLE STORY

Therefore, we two young girls found each other and became the best of friends. We talked about everything, as young girls do now. We spoke of the young boys who were in the community and how they acted. We were judgmental. We complained and giggled among ourselves and thoroughly enjoyed castrating the young men in our minds (*chuckles*).

It was during this time that my young friend was adopted into the family by a couple named Mary and ben Joseph. At first she was shy but soon took to their loving ways. They had a son whom we both knew. We found ourselves in our girlish ways falling in love with him, not realizing that it was a love of such purity that is little known among humanity today. My friend and I were not jealous of each other. We just confided in each other. We thought it was a game. *All right, who do you think will end up marrying him, you or I?* And then we would giggle and make some other remarks.

Then as the years progressed, the young man we had set our eyes upon started travelling with his uncle. We were not to see him for many months (*and even years*). By now we were older, in our teens. Life was difficult. Parts of it stemmed from the stern teachings of the Essenes. We were of course Jews and we had to learn the Torah and the Laws and follow them to the letter. We did this with some complaints. It is similar to your young people today. *Oh, gosh, it is Sunday; I have to go to church!* We were normal teenagers.

However, spirituality became a part of our lives. We did not view it as *religion*. It was what it was. It was our way of life. Then my friend and I separated. She found love with another man and married him, while I found no one else. I only could see the man I loved as being my husband. Every other man paled in comparison.

What made the comparison so difficult was that the man of my heart and dreams was what you would call and could have been *a male model of perfection*. His body was perfect. But what made him different was the level of his

MARY MAGDALENE'S LITTLE STORY

consciousness, the level of his heart energy. His eyes as he looked at you… You knew that was soul looking at you. You knew that **he knew you at a soul level**.

By now you know I am talking about my beloved, Yeshua ben Joseph. My dearest friend was Mariam. As it turned out **I** was the one who married Yeshua when he returned from his travels. Mariam and her husband, Nathaniel, gave us their blessings also, in joy.

So why am I telling you all of this, Readers, much of which you may already know? The point I am making is that as you move in today's world, there are so many influences, so many choices for you to make about everything pertaining to your life. I want to emphasize that your higher self knows what it is wishing you to do—what your contract is. If you are meant to marry that person, marry him. If not, say goodbye. Contracts can be renegotiated. Maybe you do not want to say goodbye. Renegotiate your contract and maybe say goodbye in the next lifetime.

These are times of decisions for you; are they not? Everything is a choice these days and certainly in this lifetime. For America, the choices are even more complicated with the fact of the election coming up. However, if you follow your heart, follow the wisdom of your soul, you will know which candidate to vote for. You will know.

I do not have much more to say. This is a short chapter but I wanted to tell you my little story in case you had not known of it. It is a story to let you know that Yeshua and I were destined to be together in that lifetime and forever. He is my Twin in every way; he is my heart and he is my love forever more. I AM Mary Magdalene and Lady Nada combined. Greetings. *(…an endearing story and endearing times.)*

CHAPTER 22- ANDROMEDA REX- ANGER

Good morning once again everyone, we are all here and I AM Yeshua. This Channel cleans the energy of her aura and releases any chords from the chakras just before she gets ready to bring forth a new chapter. She says a prayer; she thanks God; she thanks us. She is laying a foundation, you see. That is why you feel the energy of the books because of the foundation that she has laid.

When anyone on the spiritual path teaches, writes books, or leads groups, there always needs to be a foundation laid. It is then through that person's energy that others are drawn to him or her. The foundations are always grounded in truth and consciousness, spirituality, love and peace, Light, forgiveness—all those attributes, all those virtues are within the pages of these books.

Some people sleep with them under their pillows in order to feel the energies, not knowing that they only need to voice the intention to connect with God—All There Is, and the various Masters in order for them to make a connection with Him. It is your intention that must be voiced because this is a world of free will. Therefore, you voice your intention to do something or your intention to ask for something and then we in the other dimensions in the higher realms are allowed to answer you. That is a hard one for people to realize that they must ask for whatever it is that they are intending to manifest in their lives. Just ask and you will receive.

This chapter will be an interesting one for we are bringing in a Being of long ago and he will have much to say for his teachings today. Without further remarks from me, I shall step aside and let him come forth.

Good morning once again to our Readers. Some of you

ANDROMEDA REX- ANGER

know me while others may not. I am known as **Andromeda Rex**, and I come from the star system of Andromeda. You may be feeling surprised for you may think, *what does he have to say?* Some have not even heard of me and yet, dear Readers, I was introduced to you in the previous book (*Your Space Brothers and Sisters Greet You!*). I help the Galactic Command. I help guide humanity, although they may not know it.

Our teaching today (and I say *our* because we always come with our fellow Masters of Light) is one that you have heard before but perhaps has a different twist on it. How many times, dear souls, have you felt tremendous anger and you do not quite know what to do about it? It can come up in your dreams where you are beating someone. You wake up and are puzzled for you did not even know that person in this lifetime. You question yourself as to why you are hitting that person with a stick. *What is going on here? I would never do that in this lifetime.*

We say to you that you are releasing old hurts, old energies, and old angers that you have held within your cells from past lives. The person who you were beating is merely a catalyst. You may call him or her a *catalyst angel* who provided you a cast-member of your particular play. Therefore, you have these dreams where you are beating someone who is merely a symbol for you as a way for you to express that anger so you can release it. The energy coming upon the planet is such that you are getting in touch with what is known as your *authentic self*. The Master Kuthumi through Michelle Eloff from South Africa teaches much on this, and you can obtain more information from her website (www.indecontent.com).

This new energy coming onto the planet is a catalyst energy in itself in that it can clear your *attic*, we will call it— your attic where you have kept your darker emotions at bay. Kuthumi calls your authentic self a wild and uncompromising part of you, the part of you that speaks truth.

ANDROMEDA REX- ANGER

How can one go forward if one cannot release that pent-up emotion and redirect it, transform it? Psychologists have said many times that anger can be a catalyst in itself if it is used correctly, for it can motivate you; it can give you an impetus to move on something. If you become angry enough about a situation, do you not change it?

Some times that anger is directed at religious dogma. But unfortunately, Fundamentalists use that anger for self-righteousness. They dig their heels in and refuse to change a belief, and they become angrier about it for they think that the other person is wrong. They think the other person does not have any correct answers. They wish to hold to their concept that your Jesus was crucified. They wish to hold to the concept that he is your Savior.

However, he has expressed many times in these books that he saves no one. Only your soul can save you. Therefore, the Fundamentalists become angry and they damn humanity and are convinced that that is the devil speaking. It must be the devil in people to have them deny the Savior. However, what they do not realize is that people are not denying the Lord Jesus/Yeshua/Sananda. They are merely seeing him in a different role. How many times have you put your own ideas, your own speculations upon a person and then found that that is not true at all as you got to know the person?

That is what is going on—the speculations, people's projections upon others in order to make that person into the likeness that he or she believes ought to be. Therefore, the rage and anger builds in people until it needs to be released, for the authentic self is nothing but truth. It is uncompromising. It will not be angry over something that is not true. Your authentic self does not embrace falsehoods. People are afraid of their true nature, for they believe that that is not acceptable in society.

Let us think of it this way, if your authentic self is in truth, do you not think that you also would be in Light and love? Is not truth part of love? They are connected. If you are love, you are Light. They are connected. People need to look at themselves truthfully—to look at their shadow parts truthfully. If they see anger there, then look at that anger. *What am I really angry at?* Am I really angry at one of my relatives? Or am I really angry at the fact that I did not live up to my own expectation?

The authentic self does not project its ideas, its feelings, and its emotions onto another. Your authentic self is more connected to your soul than you realize. Do you think your soul could be connected to a part of you that is in illusion? Of course not, for your soul connects to truth.

Now I realize there are some souls that are dark, but we will not go into that at this time. Those are darker energies of the Cabal who love illusions, who love causing havoc among humanity and keeping it in fear. Those are not the souls of which I am speaking. I am talking about the souls who are searching for truth, not realizing they are searching for their authentic self—the true self, the one to which the soul can connect.

Therefore, if you have had a dream where you are beating someone with anger, just know it is your releasing some of the anger that you held from past lives and brought forward in order to transmute it. You were unable to express it in the present for that is not your nature. You are not an angry person. It would not occur to you to go around beating anyone. Therefore, how does this anger get released? You release it through your dreams. You create symbolic figures in your dreams that you think are going to harm you. Thereby, you grab a stick and beat him or her and hence release some of that anger.

Are these Beings to be feared? No, they are a gift from the subconscious. Your dreams are a gift for there is much information that lies just below the surface of your conscious self. Therefore, anger can be a catalyst for change; it can be a part of your karmic garbage that you have brought forward so that you can transmute; it can be a legitimate emotion. Would it surprise you to know that the Masters feel anger? However, they feel it in a true, clean way and they recognize it for what it is. They can make choices around it. They can decide whether to act on that anger or to transmute it or to deflect it. They know how to do that. *(They do not displace their anger on others.)* But realize that all of these ascended Masters have had Earth lives and have experienced the emotion of anger. They know it; they know what it is; they know how to react with it, to control it, or to use it in a positive way.

This is all part of honing one's character. There are other emotions that are less desirable. How about hatred? Do any of you hate something or someone? Hating is a dark emotion. It is not desirable because so often if you hate someone, you have made a judgment that that person is hateful and wrong without taking into consideration what that person's contract may be.

You read about the different murders that are going on throughout your world, and you hate that person for committing the murder. But is that his soul contract with the person he murdered? And why did they have such a contract? Could it be because the roles were reversed in a previous lifetime? The murderer and the murdered have exchanged roles, perhaps.

As you progress in your upward evolution, keep in mind that from now on anything that you feel needs to be looked at to see if it is a true emotion coming from your authentic self or if it is an illusion coming from a projection of what you would like it to be. Look at the spiritual contracts. You may not be able to read them, but know that they are there. You may not have the whole picture that you are judging and hating. You may not have the whole picture of what is going on.

ANDROMEDA REX- ANGER

You have heard that phrase, *as above, so below; as Heaven, so Earth*. Remember, you do not know what those agreements are. From now on, whenever you are feeling emotions about something, immediately think in terms, *oh, I wonder what that agreement was*? Then ask God to bless them no matter what is going on. Now in the blessing it does not mean all will kiss and make up. It merely means that you are giving it over to God, for God has all the answers. He is the One who will know what the agreements were.

I AM Andromeda Rex and I come to you this morning to help you evaluate your emotions that are arising as you come into contact with your authentic self, as you reach for that part of you that has no illusion, that is not afraid but is wild and truthful. Be your authentic self versus being in your illusions, the dream world that is not true. I leave you now.

Namaste

CLOSING STATEMENTS- YESHUA- MARY MAGDALENE/LADY NADA

Good morning precious one and to all of our Readers, we are bringing this book to a close this morning. It may take a couple of more sittings, but we will be making our closing statements. I would like to start off since I am already here.

I AM Yeshua, a son of God such as all of you are. I came into this world to help awaken humanity, to bring new energies onto the planet. It is in the eyes of the beholder to say whether I was successful or not. However, I must say that it is astounding even to me to know that something must have seeped forth from all of my efforts, for humanity knows me still. Some accept me while others do not. That is all part of the process. That is all part of the progression of history— or as some say *his-story/her-story.*

I come this morning for we are drawing our book to a close. It has been the greatest of pleasure to come several times a week and to bring forth other Masters who gladly gave you a bit of their teachings. In some respects that has been difficult because humanity is winding it up in this third dimension. Everything has a beginning and ending, the Alpha and Omega, the ending of cycle, and as you know, the year of 2008 will soon be drawing to a close. We will say that you are two steps forward to 2012.

I wish to reiterate that there is nothing to fear. The date of 2012 is simply a date where there will be a paradigm shift in consciousness and life will continue, for it would soon be 2013. But the world is not going to end! I emphasize that for any of you who may have a tad of fear remaining. This new shift in consciousness is being called the *Golden Age.* It is when people come from their hearts, from their love for others. We have said before that it is **not** me, myself, and I. It is **we** and you, my neighbor.

The year 2012 is just a date, for one cannot completely stop and change an energy flow. It is similar to a river that is flowing rapidly and then as the path narrows, it becomes a stream and then it may gradually become a lake. However, you can never stop it unless you are determined to build a dam. Energy is similar; the energy will keep flowing.

However, there will be subtle changes. The energy will be filled with more Light and love. It will flow more swiftly for there is less to hinder it—fewer "boulders" to dam it so that it cannot flow unhindered. These are all metaphors, I know, but they are intended to help you form a picture of how energies will make these changes. All will flow more swiftly and the "waters" will be more pure and clear and travel through 2012 and keep on moving forward.

Everything is speeding up as you have been told, so it will be a swifter flow. I have said before that there will be a time in your lives when you will have to make decisions, when you will need to make choices. Those choices will either propel you forward or keep you back. It is your free will given to you by the Creator—your free will to make the choice as to whether you wish to flow in the Light or whether you are going to be one of those recalcitrant Beings that gradually becomes a puppet of darkness. If you are straddling that fence, now is the time to think long and hard, for a decision must be made. You already have that decision in your heart. It is up to you whether you will follow your heart or whether you will follow some thought forms that are not of the Light that you have picked up along the way.

In this day and age, time is of the essence. You have linear time on this planet. It has been said that *time waits for no man/woman*. You have these different sayings such as *time marches on*. The age of your bodies suggests that it has been marching along with time. As you settle into your

YESHUA- MARY MAGDALENE/LADY NADA

senior years, it is a time of reflection where you begin to look back on what was and to what is now.

This Channel frequently remembers those *innocent times*, as she puts it, in her childhood. On more than one occasion she and a girlfriend would run across the street to the church; sneak up the stairs to the balcony and hang over the railing in order to watch a wedding. They were discreet and caused no trouble. The pastor took great delight in their innocence—innocent times, beloveds.

Now she is writing these books as the Masters come in and give of their wisdom. She listens and speaks into a recorder and then types it up, knowing that she then will pass the files onto her publisher to put into book form. They are then offered to all of you. It is our greatest joy to be a part of that process. She is not the only one in the world doing this. We speak through hundreds of Channels, as you know. They are dear to us, as are all of the Readers. We have no favorites for we love all—we love all. This book was an act of joy on our parts, of giving, and it is hoped that you read the material and let it give you a different slant on a teaching of which you have not thought, perhaps. Let it sink in. If it does not resonate with your belief systems, then look at those beliefs and see if something needs to be changed. We stand by our words. Can you stand by your beliefs? If they do not agree with our words, do you think there could be some changes that could be made? Of course there is that saying *we can agree to disagree*. No one needs to think like another person but there needs to be a common thread of truth in there. However, maybe yours is stated somewhat differently.

I bless you, Readers, and I am most delighted to say that we have concluded our seventh book. Of course there is always the next thought from you. *Will there be an eighth book?* And I can only say *maybe*. In the past I have said *YES*, but this time I am saying *maybe*, for it depends on what will be coming forth in this Channel's life. She will have other projects that she is not quite aware of yet. They may take her focus for a time being. One of those projects could be writing a book but different from what she has ever written. Therefore, we shall see what will happen. We will not give too much more information for she needs to awaken to it.

I will step aside and we will have another Presenter come forth to make her Closing Statement. We will then continue with other statements at another time.

Thank you, Yeshua. You are welcome, our dearest one.

Good morning, I guess this will be my last statement for this book. **I AM Mary Magdalene/Lady Nada**, coming to say my last words for all of you for this book. Of course we always say it has been our greatest pleasure to be of service to you. I hope you do not take that statement lightly, for we come with such joy and love. It is my wish for you that you feel that energy and know that it is truth that I speak.

We have spoken on quite a few topics. This morning I have no particular theme but merely want to say a few words. I wish to give you statements of *hope,* for these next few months could prove quite difficult for you. When we come to the close of a year, sometimes things escalate—that which has been in the *pipeline*, shall we say. There can become a period of time where it will be difficult for you in America. However, always know that all things shall pass. Therefore, anything negative too shall pass.

Always have hope in your heart. Always know that God is with you. Always know that you can call upon your angels, Archangels, Masters, Lady Masters, and Goddesses. You have a whole entourage that you can call upon— your Teachers and guides. Never forget that. You have an entourage of helping Souls ready to be asked. Whether you know it or not, see them or not, makes no difference, for they see you and they hear you. They know your heart and they will immediately set to work to help you in any way that they are allowed to for they will always honor your free will. Just know that and take heart. Stay in peace; find joy in everything you do. Give thanks for your abundance for there is no lack. That is a mind-set. Remember that. And you can always change your mind-set.

My love goes out to all of you. Blessings, blessings.

Thank you, Lady, thank you for all of the messages that you have brought forth making this book a gem in itself. You are welcome, precious sister, you are welcome.

All right, dear one, this is it for today. See you in a few. Greetings.

CLOSING STATEMENTS- SAINT GERMAIN- BLESSED MOTHER

Good morning once again dearest one, we are back to keep chugging on for the conclusion of this book. Now it is our greatest pleasure to have the next Presenter come forth and make his concluding statements. I step aside for this great soul.

Good morning to you dear Channel and to our Readers. **I AM Saint Germain**. I have come to say just a few words, or paragraphs, for the book is coming to a close. Everything ends cycle; everything comes to a close. Since this book is no different, this book too is ending. However, Readers, always keep in mind that the energies do not stop. They keep flowing. They merely keep flowing at a swifter pace or at a slower pace, or with more Light, or with less Light. But the energy always keeps flowing. With this book we say that it is flowing swiftly and with ever increasing Light.

It has been my greatest pleasure to come and say a few words here and there. Whether you actually read those words or not, does not make a great deal of difference. For what you are doing as you hold the book is picking up the energy that I am infusing into the pages as do all the other Presenters that have come. Our energies stay within the pages as we infuse them with love and Light, since that is who we are. Consequently, that is what you will receive.

It has been told to you many times that you are love. And yet people still associate love with an emotion. The love I am speaking about, what we have written in the book is beyond emotion. It is essence; it is the love essence. That is what we were all created with, including you. We were created with love. Therefore, that is who we are. We are love. Since love and Light cannot be separated and are synonymous I can also make the statement that this book is not only flooded with love, it is flooded with Light.

When you speak with a person and feel a loving heart, you are also feeling their Light. Thereby, you know that they carry a great deal of Light. You can speak with other people and their heart has been shut down so that they are not coming from pure love, nor do they understand it that fully, for they associate it with emotions and sexual innuendoes. However, they are love. They just do not know it yet. It (*the reality*) will come as they awaken. It will come. However, it may not be in this lifetime for them, for some are more slow to awaken, versus others.

We keep talking about 2012 and you keep reading about 2012 but we have said it is merely a date. However, at the same time it is a date of very potent innuendoes and meanings for it is a time when people will be making their ascensions into other dimensions. Now that does not mean that all of those people will be leaving the planet—will be dying, maybe in your way of thinking—but it merely means that they have raised their vibratory rate enough so that they are operating in another dimension.

We have said before that this Channel writes her books from a higher dimension in order to have contact with us. And yet she is not dead; she did not have to die in order to do so. She is conscious enough to know that she needs to raise her vibrations with intent and then maintain that vibration so that her consciousness remains in the higher dimensions. Humanity will do this eventually, but there are many Light workers who are already in the fifth dimension and touching the sixth.

However, there are layers within layers—strata—of consciousness. Even Lightworkers may be conscious on one level and not conscious on another level, for they had not awakened to that other, we will call it section, of their body consciousness. But it will happen. Once you have awakened or have trod the path it will lead you further and further into higher consciousness. It will lead you.

Many have their faith tied up in religiosity, in dogmas not realizing that those can be such a hindrance. That can be a heavy load to carry and they do not realize it for their faith is so mixed up and ingrained in erroneous belief systems and misinformation. These books, all of these books, have a purpose of awakening the Readers to different realities, awakening to different ways of thinking and approaching a new idea.

The densities of your world make it very difficult for people to rise above the density of the various thought forms that surround you and surround this Earth. Those thought forms are not real! They are exactly what their name proclaims—simply thoughts that people have repeated until they have formed an actual energy form. But they are not real. They are an illusion and they can be transmuted. They can be transformed so that instead of a million thought forms all on the same wave length, why not transmute those and have them all projecting love? Would that not be a tremendous accomplishment—to see nothing but love circulating your planet?

Keep in mind Readers that all of you are dear to my heart, for many of you channel me. So keep in mind that love is who you are. When you hear of wars and different countries invading other countries, trying to keep control in order to steal others' resources, just know that that is the last gasp of the dark forces, which we call the *Cabal*. They are fighting to the end, refusing to acknowledge that peace, love, and Light are the components of this planet and not wars and guns so that no one is safe from being attacked by their weapons. The dark forces walk country roads, streets, schools, and churches. No one is safe now for it is the last gasping breath of the Cabal (*hoping to gain control over you and/or to do away with you*).

SAINT GERMAIN- BLESSED MOTHER

You our dear Readers are most likely not in that category for you would not be drawn to read these books. However, it is time to keep a strict vigilance now wherever you go. If you are a habitual person who always does a certain activity, for it is a certain time of day in which you have always done that, change the time period; change your habit so that the dark energies cannot make plans around you in order to do harm simply because they know that you always walk or drive down that street a certain time of day.

The Dark like *creatures of habit*. It makes it easy for them to arrange so called "accidents". Be aware; be vigilant. This is the time for staying alert, for we are going into a new dimension. Therefore, it is the time when the dark will fight the hardest, will be the sneakiest and could be the most harmful. Call upon your angels, guides, and Teachers and listen. Do not be so arrogant and think that no harm will ever come to you. Just know that you can be greatly protected but you need to ask for it. It will not automatically happen. You need to ask for it (*on some level*).

I AM Saint Germain and I come to you to help close the chapters of this book, to validate that you are love, to emphasize that you need to stay vigilant; you need to stay conscious and you need to stay close to your God and release old patterns; release old habits and change your ways simply because it can confuse the dark energies and it is another way for you to stay in the Light. Thank you for your time. Blessings to all.

(Thank you Saint Germain and thank you for all of your contributions for this book.) You are welcome; you are welcome.

*Yeshua: all right, dear one, are you ready for another one? (Yes, but just let me check the batteries here. OK, it seems to be recording all right.) OK, let us see who is next. We are going to bring back the **Blessed Mother**.*

SAINT GERMAIN- BLESSED MOTHER

Hello once again, dear children and at the same time I am supposed to say *goodbye* (*chuckles*). I do enjoy my time with you. Saint Germain has just given you a little *heads-up* here to stay vigilant and to be aware that the dark energies have their eye on the various Lightworkers. If you are a creature of habit, walk a different path with your dog. Change your time-frames so that no one can say she always walks to the post-box at 3:30. Dark energies watch and they plan. Therefore, by changing your time-frames you throw a "monkey wrench" into their plans.

The time has come when there will be many people leaving the planet. It must happen, for how else will the densities lift from Earth if the denser energies are not lifted off the planet? It is time, dear souls, to make your decisions, as we have said. It is time to jump off the fence and make your choices.

As I came here this morning, I thought about the past and of course I am always drawn back to those Biblical days simply because humanity also focuses on that time. They have put me into a box being a perfect Virgin Mother. Well, can we say that no mother is perfect? Will that shock you? I look back and there are things I could have done differently with my children, just as all of you parents could have. That is how we learn.

We make a decision to do something and then years later we realize that the decision had molded the child. If the decision had been different, the child may have done something differently also. It is so important for parents to realize not to pressure the children to become what they themselves had wished to become and had never quite achieved the goal.

I would say that that is the biggest error in parenting today—the parents wanting so desperately what they did not accomplish and wanting it for their children. Maybe it was not, or I will say most likely it was not what the child had

SAINT GERMAIN- BLESSED MOTHER

brought into his/her lifetime. That child has its own contract. There are movies about some of your entertainers and their parents who wanted them to finish college. But the young adult dropped out of college in order to sing and/or play in a band. They are following their heart, for they were not meant to be a scholar. It is a hard concept for a parent to accept and to let a child lead his or her own life.

Biblical scholars have wondered about me and my parenting with Yeshua. We were a large family and each had his or her duty, we will say, in the family household. But also it was a patriarchal society so that the men's duties were not to wash up the dishes or to lay the table. That was considered women's work. However, in our household the children were encouraged to do anything that needed doing.

Yeshua did not just sit and watch his sisters do things in the house. He was not above grabbing a broom and sweeping the floor from the crumbs of a meal. He was not above laying the plates or putting down the cups. He saw what needed doing and he just did it. Everybody was talking, laughing, and sharing. It was just getting it all done.

Yeshua also liked to cook. He would come over to where I was preparing a stew and he would have a taste and he would add this and that, getting it to his liking. We did things together. He never was shooed out of the kitchen just because it was women's work. We shared everything. As the babies came he would love sitting and holding the babies, crooning to them.

Yeshua had a beautiful voice and would sing. He also was a harpist and greatly enjoyed playing it until the strictness of the rabbis told him that that was not appropriate. That it was frivolous; that it was not being serious toward his studies. He gave up the harp just to have some peace with the rabbis. However, he loved playing it and would look fondly at it and speak to it often, for in his mind it was alive. The harp held energies, you see.

SAINT GERMAIN- BLESSED MOTHER

Therefore, we look back on the lives of our children and note where we could have done better. It makes most parents sad to see where something needed to have changed and they did not do it. Each family has its own dynamic, its own personality, and its own way of doing things. Each family is doing the best that it can with the consciousness that it has at the time. And that included the quote "Holy Family" unquote.

We were a family of love and joy. However, we did follow the Laws to the best of our ability. But we were normal in all aspects of what one could call a normal family. The children would come and gather around Yeshua for he was a great story teller and he could tell stores at the level at which the children were. Even we adults loved his stories and we also were puzzled sometimes as to the meaning that he was conveying.

Today, dear Readers, keep in mind that nothing is set in stone. You can change your belief systems; you can change your habits. Try on a different belief; try on a different way of doing things; try different foods. Some people will not eat certain foods for the belief system is so strong that says *I don't like it!* Now as far as eating fried scorpions on a stick like the Chinese do, I too would draw a line at that (*chuckles*). However, carry some common sense, Readers. Make changes where you can.

I AM Mother Mary and I thank you again for allowing my time with you. Blessings, dear ones.

Thank you Mother Mary, thank you for your beautiful words throughout this book.) You are welcome, dear daughter.

OK, dear one, we will have a couple more Presenters in the next sitting and that ought to about do it. We have noticed you have started to write and edit some of the areas that all authors need to do—your title page and other separate files.

SAINT GERMAIN- BLESSED MOTHER

It is coming together. Do not feel rushed in sending this to the publishers. Take your time in the editing so that you do not have to recall it (the proof book) having left something out like you did with the previous book. Take one step at a time. We will be back in a few days.

Greetings.

CLOSING STATEMENTS- LORDS KUTHUMI- SANAT KUMARA

Good morning dearest one and to our Readers, today is the last time that we will be bringing you Presenters in order to give their closing statements. It still will be a few weeks before you Readers will be able to buy the book, for there is still much to be done—what we call the logistics of it, getting all the files in order and sending them off to the publisher.

However, today we are bringing forth the last two Presenters. Therefore, I will step aside now and let the next one begin.

Good morning to all, **I AM Kuthumi**. *(Kuthumi may I check you out please?)* This Channel has just checked me out to be sure I AM who I say I AM. And again, **I AM Kuthumi, Chohan of the Golden Ray of Love and Wisdom**. In the past we have given you words of our wisdom and of course they are infused with our love and therefore, with our Light. That is the way of all things that progress and make history—the ending of cycle—the ending and the beginning, the beginning and an ending, the constant flow of the Continuum.

Since you are close to reading the last pages of this book, as you hold it in your hands, think back on what you have learned; think back on what the various Presenters have said to you. Sometimes they often repeat, for you see, you do not have just your physical body, but your other bodies— emotional, mental, and spiritual—as well. All the bodies need to hear, feel, think, and resonate with the information on all levels. Thereby, when we speak and the information does not flow to one body, the other bodies will receive the knowledge and understand it. That is how you retain memories, for it is repetition that makes wisdom.

Also your belief systems enter into this, and if you do not believe or resonate with something that we and others have said, you will quickly set it aside and perhaps forget it. But actually it is not forgotten, for it is stored in your subconscious and will always be there until you retrieve it. I believe you have heard that *when you receive information, you receive it on many levels.* That is what is being reiterated here. You receive information through all the different bodies that your soul has in this lifetime. Your soul then can retrieve it and make it conscious to you.

We have told you in the past that all is flowing. All is on the Continuum. That is why you can bump into another concept that you may have heard two hundred years ago and then the concept comes forth again. Everything is continuing on the Continuum.

This book is a little gem in that it holds so many aspects of wisdom. We strongly suggest that you re-read it before you pass it on to others, if that is your intention. Some books are meant to be kept in one's library. Other books are meant to be passed on. These books can serve that dual purpose, for you will retain the knowledge if you can resonate with what has been said. Hold the books; feel the energy; resonate with the messages after each chapter. See if you can put the teachings into one or two lines. See if you can read a deeper meaning in the material. See if your belief systems need changing in any way.

The world as you know it is changing. If you were to pass on into Nirvana today and then come back say fifty years from now, which many of you may be doing, you will not recognize your world. The air will be cleaner. The birds will be more joyful; animals will not be so ferocious. Many of them still will maintain their previous dispositions, but they will not kill each other. That is past. People will not be eating meat. That is past. They will find other sources of proteins.

Houses will be shaped differently. There will be fewer

high-rises. That is past. However, if some of the older historical buildings still are standing, then they will be just that—historical buildings. The majority of humanity will be living in more of a dome-shaped house without such pronounced angles, but more of a softer curve.

Transportation will change. The fuel for your automobiles will not be considered as such, for the electronic waves will be used; air will be used. Many of the children who are coming on to the planet now carry this information. They know what their purpose is. There will be engineers who will go to your engineering schools, such as MIT, and they will surprise their professors, for what is presently being taught would be outdated. The young doctoral students will present their theories that will blow the minds of the professors because of the brilliance of the ideas.

This is your future fifty years from now. When you think back to the 1940's, freezers were just coming into production; television sets were just coming into production. There was no such thing as a cell phone or a computer. Look at how you have progressed in such a short number of years.

Much of the technology also will be provided by your benevolent star family. Many of the children coming to the planet will carry souls that have been trained in the star fleets and the souls will carry great inventions. There will be more Einsteins and more Teslas. There will be magnificent mathematicians. Sacred geometry will be taught in the schools, and they will be taught by this generation who brought in that information.

Therefore, dear souls, if you think you are going to die and then come back and recognize your world, we say you will not; you will not. However, what joy it will be, for there will no longer be weapons of mass destruction. There will no longer be the black forces conniving to see what and whom they can destroy. This will no longer happen.

Thereby, if it is in your contract to leave the Earth now, be thankful; count your blessings. Say *thank you God, I'm out of here!* And then you will really be joyful when you come back to Earth once again.

I AM Kuthumi and I bless all of you and I thank you for the time you have given to me. Adonai. (*Thank you, Lord, and thank you for your messages that you have given us throughout the book.*) You are welcome, our dearest one. You still have much work to do on this planet before you take your adieus—much work. (*Yes, I am a little puzzled as in "gosh, what do I do now?"*) We would say to relax and enjoy the ride. It will be one of your most involved, thrilling, and dramatic years of your life...till we meet again, our dearest Channel, blessings. (*Thank you Kuthumi.*)

All right, dear one here comes our last Presenter and then I will be back. (All right.)

Hello once again to this Channel and to our Readers. **I AM Sanat Kumara** and I have come before to give you some of my wisdom from my ancient worlds, ancient of days. I wish to reiterate some of what the Lord Kuthumi was saying to take the information; really study what has been said; take it to heart; integrate it, for unless wisdom has been integrated, it only remains as knowledge.

There are steps one takes to acquire wisdom. The first one is *intention* that you are going to study something; that you are going to acquire knowledge. The second step is that you *listen* to what is being told to you, what you are reading. The third step is to *integrate* it into all of your bodies so that all of your bodies are on the same page. And then it becomes your *wisdom—the last step*.

Of course this can happen in quick procession, while some wisdom takes a lifetime to learn. However, all wisdom is considered precious in our eyes. It is gathering *pearls* and *diamonds* of quality. It is becoming part of your makeup, part of who you are. They give the term *Master* to people who have acquired a certain expertise in something. The Ascended Masters each carry a certain expertise. Not all Masters have the same level of knowingness, of knowledge and wisdom. They had to learn this also.

Therefore, if God wishes to send a Master to do a certain task, He picks one who carries the particular frequencies He is looking for in order to create what it is that He is wishing to have done. And of course there is free will; and of course the Masters have their hands raised and are volunteering. That is more or less a *given* among the Masters who feel greatly blessed when God says to them *will you go do this for Me?* It is a blessing to be chosen.

You have heard on your teleconferencing calls and perhaps in various classes that particular groups of people, quote, unquote, have been *chosen* for a task. Now if they are as special as is being led on that they are, they will not go into ego. They will be filled with joy, for they will know that their purpose for existing has come into fruition.

And you can belong to different chosen groupings. We always feel that the designation *chosen* can be a curse or a blessing, for the person who is chosen must then live up to that standard. It is a blessing because we are not alone. We have many who are helping us. There is the whole Angelic Kingdom that we can call upon who are just as joyful to be among the chosen ones.

Whenever you hear that phrase, *the chosen one*, be sure you do not take it lightly and be sure to watch your ego, for when you are in a physical body, it is the ego that can stop you from being a chosen one, from living up to the expectations. Be aware that when God chooses you, there is an expectation that you will have integrity and that you will do the job with the utmost of your ability with love and humor and certainly without the feeling of importance. It is so important to approach your task with humility. **You** can know that you have been called to do this. **You** can know that you carry the requirements, but it is not for you to broadcast just how special you are. It is not up to you to tell the world that you have been chosen.

You all have heard that *pride goeth before a fall*. Stay humble in your task. Be accepting of others' input so that you can make the proper decisions. How would you know whether to change something if you had not listened to someone else who may have had a different perspective of what is required? Be open to new ideas; be open to change.

Now since this is the conclusion of this book, I wish to give a message to America. I wish to tell to America that this coming election of November 2, 2008, is one of the most important elections that has ever been held. It is a crossroads. Both candidates say it is a time for change. Both candidates are sincere in their belief that they can lead the nation forward with change.

It is up to you, America, to use your discernment and ask yourself what are the changes that you would like to see happen? One of the candidates is an old statesman. He has proven himself with courage, having been a prisoner of war for many years. He has proved himself in being steadfast and worthy of such a responsibility.

The other candidate is younger. He has more energy; he's articulate with a brilliant mind. Hr has not fought in wars. He has only served a short while in the Senate, but he is a fast learner and he has a great heart. That is sometimes hidden because of the turmoil of running for office.

Who will make the better President? We know but it is up to you, America, to really discern and ask yourself the important question—who do you wish to lead the Nation? One man came into this world for the only purpose of leading this nation, of being President. Which one is it? It is for you to decide.

LORDS KUTHUMI- SANAT KUMARA

We bless you now and we bless this book. Well done, dear Channel, well done.

I AM Sanat Kumara

(*Thank you Lord for your pearls of wisdom.*) You are welcome.

Dear Readers, this is Yeshua again. You have heard the concluding statements from several Presenters that have come forth. We officially bring this book to a close, but your task is still at hand, for they are suggesting that you re-read the pages and clearly understand what is being conveyed to you, to clearly understand your task which is changing any belief systems that need changing and incorporating knowledge into wisdom. This is a process that all books similar to ours present to you. Pass the book around for others to read.

I now turn this over to this Channel for the final pages that she will need to write. It has been our greatest pleasure, Readers, and our blessings go out to all of you.

We are Yeshua, Sananda, Mary Magdalene, Lady Nada, St. Germain, Lord Kuthumi, Quan Yin, Lord Ashtar and that is just to name a few who are here.

We bless you, greetings.

All right, dear one (sidebar), it is now up to you to put it together and get it off to the publishers if that is your desire. We will not say that we will be channeling an 8th book, but something different will present itself to you—something different.

Please sit once or twice a week and give us a chance to chat with you, for we always have much to say, as you know. Greetings, dear one, and our love to you.

EPILOGUE

Dear Readers, on August 21, 2008, Yeshua transmitted his last remarks for this book. I always feel somewhat of a *let down* as it slowly sinks into my body that the seventh book is finished. *The Masters' work is done.* I know there is still much for me to do before the book is ready to send to the Publishers. However, for me, just having the Masters come close enough to give me their Teachings was such a blessing. Who wants to give up being blessed every week (*smile*)?

Before I send the work on to the Publisher, I re-read every chapter. It may have been a few months since I had last read that chapter, and I am always amazed at what they had said. It is as though I am seeing it through a new lens. I feel their energies. It brings up memories of the channeling. I critique the messages. I invariably remark *gosh, that's not bad*, taking a wee bit of credit for bringing in the information (*down ego!*)

People always want to know if there is a next book; what I will be doing next. I honestly do not know! It is one of those times in my evolution where I need to have an open door in order to allow a new beginning; for what, I do not have a clue. I practice the *Law of Attraction* and I watch my thoughts and what I could be creating. Right now I am not focused on another book. Maybe it is because we will soon be into the holidays and I will have other interests, as will all of you. Thank you for your loving interest in the Masters' works. They do watch over us and know us well. Blessings,Chako.

APPENDIX- Review of God's Book

And Then God Said... Then I Said...Then He Said

A Book Review by Chako Priest, Ph.D.

This is a nonfiction, spiritual book of 236 pages. It is information that God transmitted to Celestial Blue Star of the Pleiades, David of Arcturus, and Suzanne Ward (Suzy). God spoke separately to each author about a particular issue. The authors then collaborated with their material and created 12 mind-provoking chapters that lead one into one's own belief systems to either embrace once again or to delete forever more. The theme of the book is to lead the reader step by step into a higher consciousness, a higher awareness of God's World—His truth.

The authors state that *the words of God have not been altered by us in any way.* Many people who read that statement will question still as to whether God can be channeled or not. God makes it clear in the Introduction when He states to Suzy Ward that *the parts of this book ascribed to me (God) are my words and mine alone, my messages that I gave to these dear souls to pass on to you.* The reader then is led page by page through the lens of God as He gives His answers to the probing questions from the authors.

In the second chapter God tells Suzy *however paradoxical as it may seem, the only constant anywhere is* change. He goes on to explain that the Creator—the ruler of the Cosmos, all of the Universes—gave humanity free will. Therefore, the Universe ruler, God, has to obey that—*stay out of your soul parts' choices!*

There has been much distortion down throughout history about Jesus and Mary Magdalene. God sets it straight on pages 30-31, for those of you who have always wanted to

211

know the true facts about the Crucifixion. For me, that was like a *carrot,* leading me deeper and deeper into the book, wanting to know more of what God had discussed and/or refuted next.

For you mental health servers, as well as for the layperson, God, received by Celest, gives an informative chapter on the *psyche* and *psychosis.* Celest asked God whether the psyche can heal itself after the person has passed over from the physical life. God shows His humor as He suggests thinking of the psyche as an off-world version of the Energizer rabbit. *It just keeps going and going.*

God through David links religion with politics and thinks of them as a twosome. He states that *religion and politics play upon your fears, further feeding the fear frenzy and creating insatiable desires. There is no difference between the two. Both are money-based, power-thirsty, and greed- induced.* It is statements like these that have the reader questioning, questioning as to whether one is hearing truth—whether it is really God speaking. It may create a cognitive dissonance within yourself where you will need to make a choice between outdated perceptions of your truth or your willingness to change and accept God's truth as told by these authors.

As with any well-formulated book, God's answers will raise many more questions for you. This is a book you will wish to read more than once, for the information addresses many issues of the present times—religions, politics, homosexuality, change, communication with God, and the book even discusses the year 2012.

There are special messages from Blue Star, Matthew, Serapis Bey, and Mother Mary to name but a few. They round out the information in this extraordinary book. There will be times when the reader will need to remind him or herself that the words are by God, for not everything that is spoken will be in agreement with one's own belief systems.

Review of God's Book

It then becomes one's chance to embrace God in the fullest or to sit on top of that fence of no change.

This book is truth spoken by God to His Emissaries. It is a *must have* in everyone's personal library.

6-15-08

ABOUT THE AUTHOR

Verling CHAKO Priest, PhD was born in Juneau, Alaska, hence her name of Cheechako, shortened to just Chako by her mother, a medical doctor, and her father, an Orthodontist. Chako was raised in Napa, CA. She attended the University of California at Berkeley where she met her future husband. Upon their marriage and after his training as a Navy pilot, they settled into the military way of life. They lived twelve years outside of the United States Mainland in various places, which included Hawaii, Viet Nam, Australia, and Greece. Little did she know that these exotic lands and peoples were preparing her for her spiritual awakening years hence?

After her husband's retirement from the Navy, they resettled in Napa, California. It was during this time that she returned to school at Berkeley, transferred to Sonoma University where she earned her first two degrees in Psychology. Chako then entered the doctoral program at the Institute of Transpersonal Psychology (ITP) at Menlo Park, CA, which is now located in Palo Alto, CA. She successfully completed that program which consisted of a Master, as well as the Doctorate in Transpersonal Psychology. Ten years and four degrees later she was able to pursue her passion for Metaphysical and New Age Thought—her introduction into the realm of the Spiritual Hierarchy and the Ascended Lords and Masters.

In 1988, Dr. Priest moved to Minnetonka, Minnesota. She co-authored a program called, *Second Time Around* for those with recurring cancer for Methodist Hospital. She, as a volunteer, also facilitated a grief group for Pathways of Minneapolis, and had a private practice.

She studied with a spiritual group in Minnetonka led by Donna Taylor (*now Fortune*) and the Teacher, a group of

ABOUT THE AUTHOR

highly developed entities channeled by Donna. The group traveled extensively all over the world working with the energy grids of the planet and regaining parts of their energies that were still in sacred areas waiting to be reclaimed by them, the owners. They climbed in and out of the pyramids in Egypt, tromped through the Amazon forest in Venezuela, rode camels at Sinai, and climbed the Mountain. Hiked the paths at Qumran, trod the ancient roadways in Petra, Jordan, and walked where the Master Yeshua walked in Israel.

The time came, November 1999, when Chako was guided to move to Arizona—her next phase of growth. This is where she found her beloved Masters, who in reality had always been with her. They were **all** ready for her next phase, bringing into the physical several books—mind-provoking books, telepathically received by her, from these highly evolved, beautiful, loving Beings. Each book stretches her capabilities, as well as her belief systems. Nevertheless, it is a challenge she gladly embraces.

It is now August 2008. She just has finished writing her seventh book. Yeshua has told her that an eighth book is a "maybe" at this time. Let us wait and see what manifests.

Comments and orders:

AZCHAKO@AOL.COM

Chako Priest, PhD

15859 W. Cisa Rio Lane, Surprise, AZ 85374

ISBN 142518573-8

9 781425 185732